CONTENTS KT-592-743

COMMENDATIONS

'What a story!! I confess that I knew almost nothing of Peter Grant before reading this excellent book. I trust I will be only one of a large number who are deeply indebted to my friend George Mitchell for his industry and enthusiasm in exploring this most remarkable revival in nineteenth century Scotland. May the book be widely used to create a longing for true revival in the church in the twenty-first century.'

Eric J Alexander, formerly minister of St George's Tron Church, Glasgow

'We are indebted to George Mitchell, preacher, pastor and family man possessed of a sense of humour, as he recognises these qualities in his subject, and to George Mitchell, historian, as he sets them in the context of time and place. In doing so he enlarges our understanding of the life and influence of our forebear, Peter of the Songs'.

Ian Grant, great-great-grandson of Peter Grant of the Songs

'As a Gaelic-speaking youngster brought up in a Baptist family in Tiree, I have known the name of Peter Grant from my earliest days. He was deeply respected in my home, where his wise words and outstanding pastoral qualities were frequently mentioned by my father, Hector M. Meek, who was also a Baptist minister. Grant's Gaelic hymns were sung regularly at church 'socials' in Tiree and were commonly heard on Gaelic radio as part of the repertoires of well-known singers like Mary Morrison (later Peckham) and Calum Kennedy, in addition to local singers. Grant's hymns will remain forever as an integral part of the Gaelic spiritual heritage of the mainland Highlands, the Hebrides and areas far beyond, where Gaelic speakers have settled.

Peter Grant himself was remembered as a devoted, ceaseless preacher of the Gospel, and Grantown-on-Spey was likewise held in high regard because of his association with the town and especially its Baptist Church.

However few people today are aware of the details of Grant's life and work, and some may never have heard of him. For that reason Highland Harvester is important. It presents us with a preacher whose message was grounded firmly in the Bible as God's supremely authoritative Word. He proclaimed that message in summer and winter, often travelling long distances, until he was an 'old' man – 'old' in physical terms, but ever 'young' spiritually, and always anticipating the greater glory of Heaven. Peter Grant endured many difficulties in sowing the seed of the Gospel, but he was blessed with a great harvest in his church. When revival came, he handled and nurtured his crop with godly fear and wisdom.

It is humbling to read Dr George Mitchell's deeply moving account of Rev. Peter Grant, which gives generous space to the 'harvester' himself, as he takes us through his understanding of the grace of God at different stages of his life. There will never be another Peter Grant, because God made him for his time and place, but the God of the harvest remains on His throne, and we have much to learn from His dealings with His servant in Grantown-on-Spey. We have much to learn too from the faithfulness of Peter Grant to his God and to his calling. I pray that many will read this book, and be blessed and challenged by it. Peter Grant, being dead, yet speaks.'

Donald E. Meek, Professor Emeritus

'This is a thoroughly researched account of a remarkable work of God in the North of Scotland in the aftermath of Culloden in 1745, and the subsequent brutal Highland Clearances. The reader's interest is maintained and increased as the author recounts the life and work of Peter Grant, Baptist pastor in the new town of Grantown-on-Spey, and the truly inspiring work of God which emanated from his remarkable and Sprit-anointed ministry. I pray the book will be widely read and used to provoke many to earnest prayer for our land.'

David S. Searle, retired Presbyterian minister,
Director of Rutherford House Study Centre, Edinburgh, and
Steering Committee member of 'Forward Together' Scotland.

DEDICATION

I would like to dedicate this book, 'Highland Harvester' to all my Highland friends, especially the members and friends of Inverness Baptist Church, Castle Street congregation, whom I remember with great affection.

COVER PICTURE

Grandson William and great-grandson Ian, bringing in the hay at Ballintua, 1935.

HIGHLAND HARVESTER –
PETER GRANT'S LIFE, TIMES AND LEGACY

GEORGE J MITCHELL

1

FOREWORD

Like every other faltering soul who puts pen to paper, I ride on the broad backs of other people's elephants, so to speak. The baby elephant, in my case, came in my Primary Six and Seven classes, where my teacher Mr Tommy Thomson opened up an interest in history and poetry. The young elephant belonged to John Moncrieff, MA, OBE, the history teacher who took me through SCE Higher History, and helped in my London University BA studies. (Mr Moncrieff was the son-in-law of a Baptist minister, Rev Isbister).

I have finally hitched a ride on a massive beast nurtured by John Fisher, one of my Inverness friends, who was a member of the Baptist Historical Society, and an insatiable researcher of all kinds of churchmanship, especially Baptist affairs.

John helped me in the writing of the Inverness Baptist Church centenary booklet, and after his death John's widow, Yvonne, graciously gave me much of his research work. John was especially interested in the life of Peter Grant, of Grantown-on-Spey, and I am hugely grateful for his meticulous record-keeping. John, in turn, was deeply grateful for the help received directly from the Grant family, who gave him access to the priceless sources which form the core of this life-story. Therefore my deepest gratitude to the Grant family is twice-removed, but nevertheless sincere.

Peter Grant's story is an amazing revelation of how God in His sovereignty and providence put His gracious hand on the life of an ordinary farmer, and turned this Highland Harvester into a harvester of souls for the kingdom of God. Peter Grant became the second Pastor of the Grantown-on Spey Baptist Church. During his lifetime, he saw waves of revival blessing, which passes all the qualitative tests to use that word. He saw revival visit his church and his area, and spread beyond Grantown to far-flung frontiers overseas. Peter was a man of immense physical energy, coupled with a creative, mystical and mischievous spirit. He was greatly respected by colleagues outwith his denomination. He became the greatest Gaelic hymn-writer of the nineteenth century. He was known as PARUIG GRANND nan ORAN, 'Peter Grant of the Songs'. He was also one of the movers and shakers who argued for the formation of the Baptist Union of Scotland. I believe those who read this account of his life, times and legacy, will find inspiration and incentive, and rejoice in the doctrines of grace and the sovereignty of God.

Have you ever flown in an aeroplane over the Scottish countryside, and wondered about the seismic forces which shaped the undulating landscape? Some of them resulted from ancient glacial disruption, and others were formed as the mundane aftermath of mine-working and quarrying activities. There is a kind of parallel with the changes which occurred during the life-time of Peter Grant. It would be relatively easier to consider his life in the family or church in isolation, but it is a far more difficult, but perhaps a more rewarding, task to see his life against a world of amazing change. Peter Grant lived within a fascinating kaleidoscope of social, historical and theological changes. These included the aftermath of the Jacobite Rebellions, the clammy hand of control exercised by the Moderates on the national church, the missions of the Haldane brothers and the rise of 'The Men', an influential elite within the Church of Scotland. His times were also coloured by the Agrarian Revolution, the Highland Clearances, the Hungry Forties and on the wider scale, he lived through the period of the French Revolution, the Napoleonic Wars, and the Crimean War! He was a motherless child from an early age, fathered ten children, ran a farm to feed the family, was an itinerant preacher, and pastored Grantown-on-Spey Baptist Church for 41 years!
The impact of these events, admittedly, varied in intensity for a Christian believer in Strathspey, but they illustrate the wind of change that was blowing around him throughout the eighty-four years of his life.

Peter Grant also lived through what some reputable scholars regard as the re-invention of the Highlands and the Highlanders. Before the Jacobite Rebellions, they were regarded as a filthy crowd of ungovernable savages, kept in some sort of order by their clan chiefs, 'so withered and so wild in their attire' like the witches in Shakespeare's 'Macbeth'. Yet by the mid-nineteenth century they appear as engaging, tartan-wearing, bagpipe-playing rustics, able to be marketed in Scottish souvenir shops or tins of shortbread! Furthermore, they appeared with royal approval, because by that time, Queen Victoria had bought Balmoral, and it became fashionable to employ what she called 'my dear Highlanders' as grouse-beaters or ghillies. Many of them fought and died in various wars, loyal to Queen and country.

Most importantly, in the middle of all this mayhem, here is an example of what God can do as He captures the life and guides the plough of a small-time farmer into what in every aspect constituted a straight furrow in his ministry and behaviour. This affected his large Highland family. He had eight children by his first wife, and two by his second wife, and around seventy grandchildren. He saw genuine, 'capital R' Revival. He was succeeded in the ministry at Grantown-on-Spey Baptist Church by his own son, William, and one of his grandsons, Alexander, became President of the Baptist Convention of Southern California. The reach of God's work through Peter and the church at Grantown was phenomenal, in the crop of Christian leaders, and in many other directions.

My humble hope is that you will join me in a closer look at this 'Highland Harvester'.

I am so grateful to many people for their help, especially to Margaret Cumming who made so much material available to John Fisher originally. I am grateful also to Dr Ian Grant, great-great grandson of Peter, for his punctilious reading and comment. Professor Donald Meek has been deeply involved, especially in the reconstruction of Chapter 11, since I am, sadly, a Gaelic-less Glaswegian! I have also to thank Rev Eric Alexander and Rev David Searle for their kindness, and Rev Dr Calum McInness for helpful comment. Many thanks also to Norman McDonald, History Room, Mitchell Library. Kenwil Print and Design in Kirkintilloch have again been most helpful – where Kenneth and Jim have been like mother hen. Last, but by no means least, a word of thanks to my wife Jean, for her patient endurance and constant encouragement.

SOURCES

DJ Breeze. Historic Scotland. BT Batsford, London, 1998

Jerome Burns, ed. Chronicle of the World. Longman Chronicle, Paris, 1989

Alexander Cameron. The Haldane Brothers. Heralds Trust, Edinburgh, 2001

AD Cameron. Discover Scotland's History. Scottish Cultural Press, Edinburgh, 1998

NM de S Cameron, ed. Dictionary of Scottish Church History and Theology (especially articles by Donald E Meek). T and T Clark, Edinburgh, 1993

Gerard Carruthers. Scottish Literature. Edinburgh Critical Guides. Edinburgh University Press, Edinburgh, 2009

WS Churchill. History of the English-Speaking Peoples. One volume abridgement.

TM Devine. Clanship to Crofters' War. The Social Transformation of the Scottish Highlands. Manchester University Press, Manchester, 1994

Ian Donnachie and George Hewitt. The Scottish Nation, 1700-2007. Penguin Books, London, 1999.

JD Douglas, and Philip W Comfort, eds. Who's Who in Christian History. Tyndale House Publishers, Wheaton, Illinois, 1992.

George Duncan. Preach the Word. Marshall Pickering, London, 1989.

Andrew Fisher. A Traveller's History. Scotland. A Windrush Press Book, Mackay and Co., London, 2002

MW Flinn. An Economic and Social History of Britain since 1700. Revised Edition. Macmillan Education, Basingstoke and London, 1977.

Rosemary Gorin, ed., Scotland, the Autobiography. Penguin Viking, London, 2007

James Halliday. Scotland. A Concise History. Gordon Wright Publishing, Edinburgh, 1990

RA Houston and WWJ Knox, eds. The New Penguin History of Scotland. Penguin Press, London, 2001

Tom Lennie. Glory in the Glen. Christian Focus Publications, Fearn, Ross-shire, 2009.

Carl Macdougall. Writing Scotland. Polygon. Edinburgh, 2004

Fitzroy Maclean. Highlanders – A History of the Highland Clans. Adelphi (David Campbell Publishers), London, 1995.

Fitzroy Maclean. Scotland, a Concise History. Thames and Hudson, London, revised edition 1993

Iseabail Macleod, ed. The Illustrated Encyclopedia of Scotland. Lomond, Edinburgh, 2004

M Magnusson. Scotland, The Story of a Nation. Harper Collins, London, 1982.

Donald E Meek. 'The Glory of the Lamb': The Gaelic Hymns of Peter Grant, in DW Bebbington (ed) 'The Gospel in the World', Paternoster Press, Carlisle, 2002.

'The Independent and Baptist churches of Highland Perthshire and Strathspey' in 'Transactions of the Gaelic Society of Inverness, Vol. LVI, p269-343. 'Aspects of Dissenting Evangelicals in Highland Emigration'

George J Mitchell. Guidance and Gumption. Christian Focus, Fearn, 1998; Revival Man – The Jock Troup Story. Christian Focus, Fearn, Ross-shire, 2002.

Derek B Murray. The First 100 Years. Baptist Union of Scotland, Glasgow.

Michael Newton. Handbook of the Scottish Gaelic World. Four Courts Press, Dublin, 2000.

Neil Oliver. A History of Scotland. Weidenfeld and Nicolson, Orion House, London, 2009.

John Prebble's Scotland. Pimlico, London, 2000

Eric Richards. Debating the Highland Clearances.Edinburgh University Press, Edinburgh, 2007.

Brian R Talbot. The Search for a Common Identity. The Origins of the Baptist Union of Scotland, 1800-1870. Paternoster Press, Carlisle, 2003.

H Trevor-Roper. The Invention of Scotland. Myth and History. Yale University Press, London, 2008.

Eric Richardson. A History of the Highland Clearances. Croom Heyn Ltd., London, 1982.

Eric Richards. Debating the Highland Clearances. Edinburgh University Press, Edinburgh, 2007

Haddon Robinson and Craig B Larson, eds. The Art and Craft of Biblical Preaching.
Zondervan, Grand Rapids. Michigan, 2005.

Stewart Ross. Monarchs of Scotland. Lochar Publishing, Moffatt, 1990

Paul H Scott, Ed. Scotland – a Concise Cultural History. Mainstream Publishing, Edinburgh, 1993.

Neil T Sinclair. The Highland Main Line, Atlantic Publishers, Penryn, Cornwall, 1998.

Tom Steel. Scotland's Story. Harper Collins, London, 1994.

Derick Thomson. An Introduction to Gaelic Poetry. Edinburgh University Press. Edinburgh, second edition, Edinburgh 1989.

GM Trevelyan. History of England. Longman, Edinburgh, 1973 (new illustrated edition).

Roderick Watson. The Literature of Scotland. Second edition, Palgrave Macmillan. Basingstoke, Hampshire, 2007

CA Whatley. The Industrial Revolution in Scotland. Cambridge University Press, Cambridge, 1997.

Terry Wilder. The Lost Sermons of Scottish Baptist Peter Grant. Borderstone Press, 2010.

George Yuille, ed. History of the Baptists in Scotland. Baptist Union Publications, Glasgow, 1926.

CHAPTER ONE –
NEW VILLAGE, NEW HOPES

Castle Grant, situated just north of Grantown-on-Spey, was built in the 16th century as the seat of the clan Grant of Strathspey, a prominent family in the area since the 13th century. It was extensively renovated in the 18th century, although today it is in a less-than-best condition.

The Grants of Glenmoriston suffered heavily when the Jacobite cause was lost at the Battle of Culloden, and seventy of them were deported to the colonies. They were part of the figure of around 1000 sentenced to transportation. Around 700 Jacobite supporters died in prison, 120 were executed, and around 1200 were killed in battle. The Cromdale Grants fought on the government side

In 1754, a bridge over the River Spey was built as a military road, which by-passed Cromdale, as part of the plan to strengthen Government control over the Highlands after Culloden.

There is a kind of prophetic picture in the library of Castle Grant. It shows Sir Ludovick Grant of Grant concentrating carefully over a plan of the village of Grantown. He hoped his dream would become a happier reality than the village of Cromdale. Cromdale had collapsed as a community, apparently because of the endemic in-fighting between two factions of the Clan Grant, in which some blood was shed and some lives were lost. This set Sir Ludovick off on another course of action…

He looked further afield than the gate of Castle Grant, where a village once stood. He had a glint in his eye towards a site about two miles south of the Castle, and at a lower level. The new town would be constructed along the side of the military road, and would be a service centre for the surrounding area, as well as a relocation point for displaced families who were being driven from the land because of agricultural changes. In that area there was a wide moor, typical of the gravel terraces of Strathspey.

The stone used for the earliest buildings in the town was whinstone or granite, dug out of the building plots, and the road in front of them. It also came, transported by horses pulling carts or sledges, from the moorland north of town. Larger boulders were split by heating them by fire and pouring cold water over them. Dressed stone was used around the doors and windows, and exterior walls were harled and lime-washed. The roofs were made from timber battens covered with wooden boards, and surfaced with slates from Tomintoul or other local quarries. The New Statistical Account of January 1842 quotes Mr Anderson, an author writing of the setting of Grantown: 'no village in the north of Scotland can compare with Grantown in neatness, regularity, and in beauty of situation.'

The area was lit up by the scintillating waters of the River Spey, set off by the glorious backdrop of the Cairngorm Mountains. Surely anyone coming to live in such a setting would think they had died, and gone to heaven? This view would be somewhat modified by the difficulties of wresting a livelihood from the difficult soil.

Sir Ludovick's dream village setting was completed by his detailed practical planning. The main plank in his design platform was a long street with a wide central square or mercat place, with each 'tenement' house having a strip of land attached. The square developed into a long rectangle of lawns with an avenue of well-established trees. The desolate moorland on which the village was built disappeared.

After an initial advert in 1764, the first house was built in 1766, but by 1768, only about sixteen feus had been taken up

The 'location, location' message went out from Grantown in a second advertisement, issued in 1768. This invited 'persons of circumstance, manufacturers, and others' to take up feus. The village had nine annual Fairs, and weekly mercats, dealing in 'Cattle, Horses, Sheep, Tissiker, Wool, etc'. Its location was eminently suitable for the South Country, The village was no more than eighteen miles from Inverness, Fort George, Nairn, Forres, Elgin, Keith or Strathbogie, with good road links throughout. 'There is established a good schoole, for teaching Latin, English, Writing, Arithmetic and Book-keeping, and two Weemen Schools for Sewing and Knitting of Stocking'. The cup of joy was complete with the news that a fine new church was to be built within the town, in 1803. The New Statistical Account of April 1841 says: 'There are no Dissenting chapels of any kind, except a Baptist meeting-house in Grantown.'

Rev John Grant, minister of Abernethy and Kincardine, summed things up like this: 'Political or religious fanaticism have got no foothold here'.

He took a paternal interest in the crofters and small farmers of the area, and encouraged the development of education. Sometimes he would abandon the customary improving sermon, and read the latest war news in the newspapers from the pulpit, with the introductory phrase: 'Let's see what Boney (Napoleon Bonaparte) has been up to.'

Sir James Grant continued and completed his father's single-minded aim and practical action, and is reported to have spent £5000 on Grantown. He constructed roads, built bridges, and erected a Town House and jail. John 'Begg' Scott, a local contractor, built the bridge over the Spey in 1754, at the same time as the military road from Coupar Angus to Fort George was being constructed. Major-General George Wade master-minded over six hundred kilometres of new roads in the Highlands

'Had you seen these roads before they were made
You would lift up your hands, and bless General Wade.'

Sir James Grant encouraged local industries, like baking, weaving, dyeing, wool-combing and brewing, 'to keep people from spirituous liquors'. Sir James consulted Lord Kames, reckoned to be an authority in education, about the curriculum for a school where instruction in skills and trades could be given, anticipating modern technical education schemes.

Lord Kames suggested that the best way forward was to attract to Grantown 'the best artists in such things for which there was a demand in the Highlands –wheel-wrights, plough-wrights, house carpenters, weavers and so on'. Lord Kames promised financial support from The Annexed Estates Fund to pay for apprenticeships in such trades.

By 1792, Revd Lewis Grant reports in the O.S. Account that Grantown had grown from 300 to 400 residents 'as good tradesmen as any in the kingdom'. He adds a moralistic rider: 'herein was irresistible proof how far the country was capable of improvement'.

There had been an abortive attempt to build a Strathspey Academy at Cromdale, and the scheme was transferred to Grantown. The original building was replaced by a fine four-sectioned building boasting a bell tower, surrounding a central courtyard to be used for drill.

The whole community grew, and cottage industries flourished. Settlers came in from a wide area, including a few from England...

The new village was beginning to look like a new town. Archimedes said: 'Give me a place to stand, and I will move the world'. Grantown provided such a place for Peter Grant.

CHAPTER TWO –
HIGHLAND HARD TIMES

Peter Grant's father was a tenant farmer, a precarious position at any time, but particularly in 1783, after the previous year's famine in the Highlands. The harvest had been a total failure, and the local people were trying to survive the winter on shares of a load of pease-meal salvaged from a wrecked ship in the Moray Firth. They had to live as the old Scots song has it:

'Pease brose, again, mither, pease brose again; feed me like a blackbird, and me your only wean…' This author remembers seeing and occasionally eating this light brown powder (split peas boiled for hours, powdered, and made into a kind of porridge with boiling water, milk and sugar) as a breakfast cereal, accompanied by mother's singing !

Any flickering hopes of Jacobite deliverance in the post-Culloden period from 1746 were finally extinguished by the death of the dissolute Charles Edward Stuart in 1788. Although Bonnie Prince Charlie had scared the life out of the English Parliament by reaching as far south as Derby in his southwards advance, there was little realistic hope that a Stuart would return to the throne of England as long as the exiled dynasty remained Roman Catholic.

There was a certain ambivalence in status and views between English and Scots from 1745 onwards.. Tom Devine writes: 'On the one hand, the (Scottish) nation's rise to prosperity depended on the new connection with their southern neighbour, but, on the other, the political and material superiority of England threatened full-scale assimilation of Scotland.'

The English opinion of Highlanders was widely that they were brutish savages, in great need of being civilised. Tom Devine quotes a contemptuous article in the January 1746 'Gentleman's Magazine' by 'a gentleman of Derby', concerning clansmen billeted in his house:

'About 6 o'clock on Wednesday evening were quartered on me six officers (one a major, as they stiled him), and forty private men…Most of the men… looked like so many fiends turned out of hell, to ravage the kingdom, and cut throats; but these wretches being fatigued with their long march from Leek that day… stuffed themselves well with (my) bread, cheese and ale. My hall stunk of their itch and other nastinesses about them, as if they had been so many persons in a condemned hole.

'Their dialect (from the idea I have of it) seemed to me, as if an herd of Hottentots, wild monkeys in a desert, or vagrant gypsies had been jabbering, screaming, and howling together; and really this jargon of speech was very properly suited to such a sett of banditti.

'I cannot omit taking notice of the generous present they made me at parting on Friday morning, for the trouble and expense I was at, and the dangers undergone, (tho' by the by I wished for no other compensation than the escape of my family with their lives, and of my house being plundered) which was a regiment of lice… and other ejections of different colours, scattered before my door, in the garden, and elsewhere about my house.'

The low view of the Highlanders was reinforced by The Rt Hon.Duncan Forbes, Lord President of the Courts of Session in Scotland. He wrote 'Some Thoughts on the State of the Highlands of Scotland' around 1746: 'The inhabitants of the mountains, unacquainted with industry and the fruits of it, and united in some degree by the singularity of dress and language, stick close to their ancient idle way of life; retain their barbarous customs and maxims…and being accustomed to the use of Arms, and inured to hard living, are dangerous to the public peace…the grounds that are cultivated yield small quantities of mean Corn, not sufficient to feed the inhabitants… Their constant residence during the harvest, winter and spring, is at their small farms, in houses made of turf; the roof, which is thatched, supported by timber. In the summer season, they drive their flocks and herds many miles higher amongst the mountains, where they have large ranges of coarse pasture. The whole family follow the Cattle; the men to guard them, and to prevent them straying, the women to milk them…the places in which they reside when thus employed they call shoelings (shielings GJM) and their habitations are the most miserable huts that ever were seen…'

He goes on to recommend setting up spinning and weaving schools, disarming the Highlanders, having preventive measures in place to deal with insurrection, and being prepared to take leases over any mines or 'improveable ground.'

Professor Hugh Trevor-Roper's view of Scottish history is that myth is central to our understanding of our history and politics. His argument states that our historical, literary and what he calls our 'sartorial past' has been re-written. He blames John of Fordun for inaccurate historical work, James Macpherson for rewriting the Irish Gaelic source 'Fingal'. Trevor-Roper also exposes what he would call 'the myth of kilt and tartan', claiming the kilt was invented by an English Quaker from Lancashire, Thomas Rawlinson, who separated the kilt from the plaid in the 1720s. The trade with England in tartan goods flourished after the post-Jacobite ban on tartan was lifted in 1782, and Trevor-Roper argues that Highlanders perpetuated the myth of an ancient origin for the kilt, which was helpful to get rid of their barbarian image.

He claims that the process of change took place between 1745 and 1845; 'Before 1745, the Highlanders and all their customs were disowned and despised by every articulate Scotsman. After 1845, the Highland takeover was complete....Romanticism might lose its power; but then tourism and commercialism would take over its legacy, extending and vulgarising it in detail. Today it is fixed in elaborate rituals of Scots abroad, and in the well-stocked souvenir shops of Lowland Scotland.'
Trevor-Roper's views are not widely popular, but deserve mention. He was Regius Professor of History at the University of Oxford.

In the Highlands, the spin-offs of the agricultural revolution were gathering momentum. The Disarming Act of 1746 and the Clan Act were followed by the building of roads, garrisons at Fort William, Fort Augustus and Fort George, and barracks at Ruthven, Bernera and Inversnaid.

There was a displacement of large numbers of people, carried out by hereditary aristocratic landlords. State action and control in the Scottish Highlands left the poor wide open to be cleared out to make room for sheep-based agriculture. The 1756 Act of the Court of Session gave landlords rights to remove tenants by applying to a local sheriff forty days before Whitsun. Many of the leases were for only one year, so in some cases landlords simply had to wait until the period of lease ran out. Sheep farming was potentially much more lucrative than collecting crofters' rent. The New

Statistical Account of 1841 mentions the West Highland breed of black-faced sheep and some Cheviot sheep in the Grantown area. It notes that the prize bull at the 1839 Inverness Highland Society Show came from the Grantown area. The Account also notes improved farming methods in the area, five and six-year rotation methods of cropping, and trenching and draining as existing in almost every farm in the parish.

The temptation in describing the Highland Clearances is to concentrate on misery and conflict. The effects were disparate, since the Clearances occurred over a long period, and were sometimes gradual in character and varied in severity.

1792 was called 'The Year of the Sheep' in Caithness and Sutherland, when large numbers of crofters and small farmers were moved out to the margins of land holdings, especially in coastal areas. They were expected to live in the open until they built houses for themselves, and to eke out a livelihood by fishing or kelp-gathering. In the Badbea area of Caithness, women tethered their livestock and children to rocks and posts to prevent them being blown off the cliffs into the sea.

Some people were put directly on emigration ships to Nova Scotia, Glengarry, and the Kingston areas of Ontario, Canada, and the Carolinas of America. In 1807 Elizabeth Gordon, nineteenth Countess of Sutherland, said of her husband Lord Stafford: 'He is as seized as much as I am with the rage of improvements, and we both turn our attention with the greatest of energy to turnips.' Stafford (who became Duke of Sutherland) brought in his first commissioner, William Young, in 1809, and soon afterwards Patrick Sellar was his factor, acting with cruelty and self-interest as he acquired his own sheep farms.

The vocabulary changed from 'enclosures' and 'encouragements' to 'evictions' and 'clearances'. In the savage and brutal clearances of 1811-1820 in Sutherland, when up to two thousand families a day were evicted, many starved and froze to death. Donald McLeod, a Sutherland crofter gave a harrowing account of the burning of around 250 houses, reporting the cries of children, terrified cattle and dogs, and the dense cloud of smoke covering a large area of land, and stretching out to sea.

The rich landowners later professed ignorance of what their factors were doing, and pointed to other improvements, like Stafford's creation of a coal-pit, salt pans, brick and tile works, and herring fisheries.

Elizabeth Leveson-Gower, Duchess of Sutherland, described her starving tenants in a letter to a friend: 'Scotch people are of happier constitution, and do not fatten like the larger breed of animals.'

The misery felt elsewhere in the Highlands had effects also in Strathspey and Grantown, and there is mention and evidence from the Grantown church of emigration to the Americas and elsewhere, and a movement overseas of good competent leaders.

Tom Devine writes: ' In a society where legal security was minimal, clearances spread alarm and anxiety, which led to preparation for emigration long before they faced the direct threat of removal.'

There was a painful dimension peculiar to Gaeldom, paralleled to some extent in some Latin American countries, the Andes area of Peru particularly. The landowner, or 'patron' was regarded as protector, as well as owner. Among the Gaels the principle is 'duthchas', which meant the landowner was assumed to be guarantor of land and property. As the concept of clanship faded into the background through the clan elite becoming absorbed in British society, the ordinary people of the Highlands were left exposed, vulnerable and worried. A few sought, or prepared for, a new life abroad, exporting with them the solidarity of a church group, and even a minister.

In the realm of ideas, there were other concerns on the eighteenth century horizon – the theological view of Deism, where God is like an absentee Watchmaker, and humans as essentially good creatures.

The Moderates were an influential elite within the Church of Scotland. They were sympathetic to these new ideas. Their views may date from William II's message to the General Assembly of the Church of Scotland in 1690: 'Moderation is what religion requires, neighbouring churches expect from you, and we recommend to you.' They supported patronage in the placement of ministers in churches, and were uneasy about supporting the Westminster Confession of Faith. In the latter part of the eighteenth century, their grip tightened, although the wealthy and privileged must have had misgivings about humanity's intrinsic goodness when the streets of Paris ran with aristocratic blood, as the Revolution became the Terror in France.

In the field of philosophy, the brilliant Scottish philosopher David Hume (1711-76) was an empiricist. He argued that knowledge was built entirely on experience and sense perception, and rejected both Deism and Christianity, especially miracle stories. The cumulative impact of Deism and empirical scepticism blunted the edge of Christian evangelism and mission, and tended to undermine any enthusiastic confidence in the Christian message.

There were good aspects to the post-Culloden pressures. Scotland gained better roads, but the main reason for this work was military. The 1746 Disarming Act, mentioned earlier, made English intentions clear. No weapons were to be carried, and breaking this law incurred heavy punishments. Tartans in plaids, kilts, trews (tartan trousers) or outer coats were banned. Bagpipes were prohibited as an instrument of war (some people, and not solely the English, could sympathise with this approach, and regard this measure as an improvement!)

There was an improvement for a time for tenant farmers in longer leases, giving better security of tenure. This improved possibilities in the long term for hedging, walling, housing and new methods of agriculture in grazing and selective breeding of livestock.

From the time of the Union of the Parliaments 1707, the Scots had access to England's trade privileges and foreign markets. Generally, we must concede that the times were grim for man and beast in the Highlands. Potatoes and porridge formed a monotonous but wholesome contribution to the Highland diet, but crop failure meant widespread starvation. There was a profound contrast between the Highlands and the South of Scotland in one direction at least.

By 1770, Scotland accounted for more than half of the lucrative tobacco trade with Southern States in America, so that Glasgow's 'tobacco lords' could 'strut their stuff' in the city centre, while Highlanders shivered and starved. The population of Glasgow had risen to 100,000 by the year 1800.

Many dispossessed Highlanders found work there and exchanged rural life for urban squalor.

Trade with the American colonies increased dramatically in Glasgow after the deepening of the River Clyde in 1776.

Farming in the Highlands area presented a formidable challenge because of the large mountainous area in the centre, separating it from the fertile lowlands of the North-East. There was little hope of imminent help through the founding of the Highland Agricultural Society (formerly known as 'The Highland Society of Edinburgh') in 1784, a year after Peter Grant's birth. The Society was a bastion of privilege. Its membership consisted of 'noblemen and gentlemen of rank, property and professional eminence'. Nevertheless, the long-term aim of the Society was very good, namely the promotion of good agricultural practice.

The 'tacksman', from the Scots 'tack' meaning 'tenure', was a key figure in Highland farming. He generally held a lease from the clan chief or land-owner. He was a factor, or middle-man, whose task was tax-farming a district so that the rent-roll was filled with loyal, and if possible, supine tenants, who filled the clan chief's coffers from vast and often inaccessible estates.

Tacksmen made handsome profits for their overlords, and generated hate and scorn during the Clearances, when they were regarded as quislings.

The period was, as Michael Newton writes: 'a watershed in the history of the Gaels, because of the finality of control which the new elements of Anglicisation had achieved'. The higher echelons of Scottish society began to view their estates chiefly as hunting-grounds for shooting parties. The tenant-farmers were aware only of escalating rents, and the possibilities of being displaced in favour of sheep, since wool and mutton could generate more money than rental income produced. The first large-scale clearance took place in 1785, when people were forcibly evicted from their homes in Glengarry. This sent a shiver down the Highland spine.

There were crop failures in the Highlands approximately every three or four years. The kelp (seaweed) industry provided a temporary means of making money, mainly in the North Highlands and Western Isles. Burning kelp produced alkalis suitable for the glass and soap industries of the urban south. Some tenant farmers had been moved to the less fertile coastal strips, where labour was needed for the kelp industry.

Unfortunately demand for kelp died during the Napoleonic wars, and efforts were made to remove tenants altogether.

Changes in the Salt Laws in 1825 had ruinous effects on the salt and kelp industry. Furthermore, the withdrawal of the need for secondary production by hand-spinners in the face of advancing mechanisation had a devastating impact on the Highlands. CA Whitley comments: 'In no part of the British Isles did market forces and industrialisation wreak so much havoc, or leave such human suffering in their wake as in the Highlands and Islands of Scotland.' There were countless numbers of congested crofting settlements with no apparent potential for economic development.

Evictions reached a peak in the 1840s after the lean years of the potato famine. Iseabail Macleod writes: 'Many evictions were carried out in a brutal and inhumane fashion, especially by the Duke and Duchess of Sutherland, and their factor, Patrick Sellar.'

Any fair analysis of the situation must consider the spiritual influence of religious revivals in the Highlands. There were increasing incidences of these after 1790, especially in the Western Isles. They may be linked to the success of the Gaelic Schools Societies' work, with its bases in Edinburgh, Dundee, Glasgow and Inverness. The movement had a main aim to spread Gaelic literacy so that Gaels could read the Bible in the 'language of the heart.' Teachers exercised a peripatetic role as reading skills improved. There were some incidences of extreme behaviour, like frenzied convulsions, wailing and fits in the Western Isles revivals. In the Strathspey area, later on, Peter Grant was very careful to exercise restraint. There were no special revival meetings. He kept things within his normal church programmes, although the numbers were large (most Scottish churches today would not be able to match twice-a-week prayer meetings with more than two hundred attending each time!). Peter Grant exhausted himself in the extent of his personal counselling, keeping abreast of what God was doing in the lives of his congregations.

Some scholars have tried to make direct links between revivals and crises like disease (for example, the cholera epidemic in the Grantown area in 1832) or clearances, famine or other physical privation, like the homelessness which was part of the clearances picture. Doubtless, the evangelical message of grace, faith and patience in the face of adversity helped to cushion the devastating impact of these things. These troubles were factors, but the dimension of the sovereign work of God in revivals cannot be explained away solely by such circumstances.

Peter Grant was born in the farmhouse at Ballentua, some three miles from Grantown. He was born into a tough school of life, where he would have to face difficult times.

CHAPTER THREE –
THE GRANTOWN BOYS GET GOING

Peter Grant's parents and ancestors had farmed about thirty-seven acres arable and about two hundred and ninety acres of hill country, including rough grazing. Peter wrote about his family: (they were) 'so strictly honest that the landlord told me, over and over, that I was getting the farm at a lower rent, because my ancestors never allowed their rent to fall in arrears, no, not for a day, as far back as could be remembered.'

Peter's parents were Donald Grant and Janet Stuart. Peter was born on 30 January 1783. Peter's mother had been known as a beautiful woman, but she was now in poor health. When Peter was three years old, he was removed to live with his grandparents at the nearby farm of Ballenluig. There has been some debate about the date of his mother's death, but it is now resolved as 17 May 1783 when Peter was less than five months old. He remained with his grandparents, the Stuarts at Ballenluig until he was twenty-two, when he returned to take possession of his father's farm. Peter tells how he was treated well, and wrote about his grandfather: 'He was an elder of the Kirk (at Abernethy), much respected, but he could not read or write.' His family religion was formal, and made a minimum impact on the daily life of the household. The family still farm Ballintua, an unbroken tenancy for around three hundred years.

Peter's widower father Donald found time somehow to improve his skills as a fiddler at local functions and celebrations. Peter himself was in great demand to play at ceilidhs, dances and weddings. These celebrations were described later in Peter's son William's 'Brief Sketch' of his father's life and labours for the Report of the Baptist Home Mission of 1868 as 'wont to be scenes of the wildest merriment'.

Sometimes families get together only at family funerals. When young Peter Grant was only twelve years old, in 1795, he was present at the family reunion which accompanied a family funeral . A stranger to Peter came to the funeral, and spent the night at Ballenluig. According to a letter sent to Mr Grant Waugh on 18 October 1951, Peter Grant's great grand-daughter, quoting her mother, identified the stranger as a friend of the Stuart family of Ballenluig, Peter's mother's family. The stranger surprised the family gathered round the peat fire when he produced a little book of spiritual songs, written in Gaelic. He began to sing the songs to the family, and won a lot of interest, because they were set to old Highland tunes. Few people around that fireside realised the impression this made on the quiet little boy in the corner. The book was Dugald Buchanan's 'Laoidhean Spioradail' ('Spiritual Hymns'). The letter of 18 October 1951 also pinpoints the key song on that night as Dugald Buchanan's famous song 'La a' Bhreitheonais' – the 'Day of Judgement'. When the visitor saw young Peter's obvious interest, he gave him the book. Peter was a thoughtful boy with an inherent love of learning. He learned to read and sing all the songs, and began to teach them to his friends.

The books we read can have a significant influence on our lives. It was no small thing in the providence of God that Dugald Buchanan's little book came into the hands of Peter Grant. Donald Meek has helpfully substantiated the important role played by Dugald Buchanan (1716-68) in Gaelic education and theology. Buchanan was a miller's son from Ardoch, in Perthshire's 'Bonnie Strathyre'. In his earlier adult life, he was a restless soul – tutor, carpenter's apprentice, and farmer. He documented his tortuous pilgrimage in a diary, which he wrote in English. He heard George Whitefield preach at the heart of the Cambuslang Revival in 1742, and found peace with God in 1744. From 1750, he settled into God's appointed role for him as a preacher, teacher, catechist, and Gaelic religious poet. In 1753, he settled in the estate of Strowan, Kinloch Rannoch, and as a teacher with the Society for the Propagation of Christian Knowledge (SPCK), was instrumental in planting schools. Donald Meek traces the poetic influences of Isaac Watts, Edward Young, and the Scottish poet Robert Blair on Buchanan's writing.

His eight surviving poems provide a solid base for his poetic craftsmanship, covering the main themes of God's majesty, Christ's suffering, impending judgement, and the heroic qualities of the Christian warrior in a transient world. His imagery draws from the topography and climate of rural Perthshire.

Dugald Buchanan's stature as a Gaelic scholar is seen in his definitive role in supervising the printing of the Scottish Gaelic New Testament in 1767, published the year before he died.

Later on, one of Peter's uncles was in Edinburgh on business, and brought him home as a gift a copy of Alleyne's 'Alarm to the Unconverted', published in a Gaelic translation. From then on, both books, Buchanan and Alleyne, were Peter's constant companions while he was herding the cattle or caring for the sheep on the slopes of the Grampians. In the 'Brief Sketch' made for the 1868 Report to the Baptist Home Mission, William Grant writes about his father's educational disadvantages: 'At the age of twelve, he could read a little English, but could not understand a word of it; and the Gaelic, his mother tongue, he could not read, and indeed had no books in it. Buchanan and Alleyne's works made a tremendous impact on him.'

Later on Peter said : 'I learnt from that book (Alleyne) the necessity of a new heart and life. Although I never saw anyone that seemed to be concerned about their soul, I began to understand that such people were in some part of the world. I wished much to see one'. God had stirred up a heart hunger for God in the heart of this thoughtful, musical, young hillside herder. Gaelic was his mother tongue, and governed his thought processes, but after some years, he acquired English, which he spoke with correctness and fluency. Like Luther, he did not see why Satan should have all the best tunes, and as his spiritual appetites grew, he resolved to do what he could to bring about a change for the better. It is curious that the Highland people, while they strongly objected to hymns in church, had no hesitation in using them in their homes. Peter Grant's 'Dan Spioradail' ('Spiritual Songs') was first published in 1809, and Peter lived to see his little book, later expanded, in its tenth edition.

In his later teenage years, Peter became increasingly involved with his widower father, from whom he acquired an interest in music, and developed the same skills as a fiddler. He was also a good singer. Like his father, young Peter became a key figure as the fiddler, playing at local celebrations. He also served as precentor (song-leader) in his local church, often leading the worship with his fiddle.

One of Peter's contemporaries was Duncan Dunbar.

We are indebted to the Strathspey Herald for an appraisal of Duncan Dunbar under the title 'Patriot and Pioneer: Rev Duncan Dunbar', published on 21 August 1924.

'Although he was about seven years younger than Peter, Duncan Dunbar became the undisputed ring-leader of the Grantown lads. Duncan was born in 1790 in a small croft near Spey Bridge, beside the old 'Wade road'. His father was a douce, unassuming man, whose hard work and frugal lifestyle enabled his children to have the best education that the Grammar School in Grantown could give. Duncan's parents produced a firecracker of a boy. In their Gaelic-speaking home, he was a devil-may-care risk-taker, and

Ballintua Farmhouse, 1983, during Bi-Centenary celebrations.

became the leader of all the fun-loving lads in the district. He was regardless of danger and a stranger to fear. He was a brilliantly co-ordinated athlete, skilful and daring. When he was a fairly young boy, he would go on the River Spey, and then dive off a boat down into the deepest water, and remain there until his terrified pals thought he would never surface again. Old people who remembered him as a boy said he was as wild as the deer on his native hills. Alex Cumming tells how he was known to catch an unbroken colt, and jump on its back, like any 'bronco-buster' in America. The scared creature would bound over hill and dale until it was utterly exhausted. The colt would then slacken its pace, and its persistent young rider, having become its master, could usually guide the beast at will.

Another of his favourite tricks put the public in a state of fear and alarm. He used to do head-stands on the parapet of the Spey Bridge, with the foaming waters rumbling beneath him.

The locals were quoted as saying: 'Sure that laddie will brak' his banes (bones)…wee Duncan will come to nae good end. E'en if his life should be spared, he'll be guid for naething but a mountebank play-actor'. His skill at games formed a strong bond between Duncan and the young son of the Laird of Grant. Duncan was a brilliant dancer, and was often invited to Castle Grant when Lowland guests were to be entertained.'

From the time he was about nine years old, Duncan was deeply affected by a local tragedy. 'The Black Officer', Captain McPherson of Ballochroan, and a Christmas hunting party he took with him, were swept away by an avalanche while sheltering in a bothy under a huge cliff. This took place on Hogmanay, in a corrie on the slopes of the Forest of Gaick, in the wilds of Badenoch. The Black Officer was hated for his unscrupulous methods of press-ganging people to fight in the American and Napoleonic wars. Local legend claimed he was in league with the devil, and that Satan had come to claim his own that fateful Hogmanay.

When Duncan Dunbar was about sixteen years old, he persuaded some bold spirits to join him in seeing the New Year in at the wild corrie of Gaick, to taste adventure and the spice of danger. They came back free from harm danger or accident, but the tragedy weighed on his mind, and was probably a factor in his later turning to God.

Duncan probably found peace with God through the help of his former minister, Revd Grigor Grant of Cromdale, but announced his intention to join 'the little band of people here who feared God', with whom he now intended to worship.

After attending some classes at Edinburgh University, and working in business and marrying in Aberdeen, Duncan Dunbar emigrated to America. On 31 October 1818, after baptism, Duncan was ordained pastor of St George's Baptist Church, New Brunswick. In the spring of 1819 a society was constituted under the name of 'the Evangelical Society of New Brunswick', embracing three religious denominations. He was designated to return to Britain to raise funds and recruit missionaries for the Society. He travelled widely, and was well received. He returned after a year with his wife and family, but after a difficult voyage their ship was wrecked on the coast of Bermuda. Eventually he reached New Brunswick. He began to minister in English, and in Gaelic for the exiled Highlanders he came across, and the others were deeply affected by their singing of the Psalms in Gaelic. An eyewitness reported that 'some aged Highlanders walked thirty or forty miles to see Mr Dunbar, so great was their love for him, and for the music of their mother tongue.'

Duncan Dunbar also served as minister of McDougal Street Baptist Church, New York. In later life he served God reviving feeble congregations in the Eastern USA, and representing the Missionary Unions of Philadelphia and Pennsylvania. His return visits to Grantown in 1836 and 1840, and the intertwining of his life and Peter Grant's were to be significant in the church's life.

In the summer of 1836, he was seriously ill, and paid a visit to Scotland and Grantown as part of his recuperation. His preaching at Grantown was accompanied by mighty blessing. On his return to New York, one of his sons-in-law said to him: 'Why do you not look a day older than when you left?' He replied with a smile, 'My son, I did not go to Scotland to grow older.'

About forty years before Abraham Lincoln began his drive for slave emancipation, Duncan Dunbar championed the cause of slave emancipation by speech and pen. He was a warm friend and advocate of the oppressed slaves in the United States. He identified fully with anti-slavery men, and became President of the New York City Anti-Slavery Society. His church would not admit to membership any slave-dealer or slave-owner.

Duncan Dunbar never forgot any act of kindness done to him. Miss Grant of Auchernack wrote to Duncan's daughter after his death: 'When your father paid his first visit to Scotland about thirty years ago, he spoke much to me, as the eldest of our family and the one he best remembered, of his obligations to our father for kindness shown him when he was a boy, and begged me for some opportunity of returning it, if ever I wished to befriend any lad.' While in America, Duncan had an ardent desire to help exiled Scots. On man testified that, 'more than any man I knew, he followed out the spirit of God's injunction: 'Ye know the heart of a stranger, seeing ye were strangers in Egypt.' He also had a warm interest in the cause of the Red Indians, or Native Americans, as they are called now. The oppressions they suffered were a great source of real grief for him.

Duncan Dunbar paid his last visit to Scotland in 1864. He sent a message to Peter Grant, now in his eighties, from the Grant Arms Hotel, and there was a joyful reunion. They swopped notes on their families. Mr Grant won on the number of children and grandchildren, but Mr Dunbar won with three great-grandchildren to his friend's two! Duncan Dunbar preached in Grantown on the following Sabbath morning, and Peter, in William's absence, preached in Gaelic in the afternoon. He contracted a serious illness, and finally passed away aged 74, on 30 July 1864.

It is awe-inspiring to consider the wide variety of character and personality God chooses to be His servants and leaders. Imagine the potent combination of the wiry workaholic herd-boy, Peter Grant, with his sensitive musical spirit, clear Biblical standards, and preaching gifts, and the boundless energy of a Duncan Dunbar, the wild young tearaway of Grantown.

They were true pioneers. People like Peter Grant and Duncan Dunbar seem a healthy contrast to some of the persons with the white suits, gold 'knuckle-dusters' and soft hands that claim to represent Jesus on our television screens and pulpits, at the present time.

Biblical meekness is not weakness, it is controlled strength, shown when people are saved by God's grace and mastered by His divine discipline. Moses was the 'meekest man on the face of the earth' (Numbers 12 verse 3). His inner identity was linked to a hated minority to be found in the slave-camps and slime-pits of Egypt, rather than its temples and palaces. Yet Moses could strangle an Egyptian and bury him in the sand! When Moses learned how to obey God in the desert of Horeb, and led a nation from 'the iron furnace' of Egypt, a place of burden, heat and pressure, God was ready to shape him to be His meek servant. The Lord Jesus Christ was also 'meek, and lowly in heart.'

Similarly, in the harsh judgemental environment they were to face in Grantown, God shaped Peter Grant and Duncan Dunbar for future leadership and usefulness, even when they shared a pulpit as great-grandfathers.

CHAPTER FOUR –
DISTURBERS OF THE STATUS QUO...

To the outward observer, the Strathspey area at the start of the nineteenth century must have looked like a calm community with settled habits. Relatively, this was the case, but across the English Channel, dark forces were at work, and massive Continental armies were on the move, and there were repercussions for Scotland. The idealistic hopes in France of replacing the 'ancien regime' with a new society characterised by 'liberty, equality and fraternity' were drowned in the bloodbath of the Terror, dominated by Mademoiselle Guillotine. People were mobilised and ready to fight for a cause. One of the Girodin ministers said : 'We have 300,000 men armed and ready to march. We must march them until they are exhausted, or they will come back and cut our throats.' All they needed was a leader, and Napoleon Bonaparte emerged from the pack to plague the rest of Europe until 1815, leaving long-term repercussions, of seismic proportions, on the future of the continent.

In Britain, the early idealism and overt support for the French revolution by people like Burke, and even Wordsworth : 'Bliss was it in that dawn to be alive, and to be young, was very heaven', gave way to hellish fears that the French disease would spread to Britain, and who was to be trusted? Some people thought armed Highlanders could give military help. TM Devine quotes a political commentator in the June 1739 issue of 'The Gentleman's Magazine': 'Some Clans of Highlanders, well instructed in the Arts of War, and well affected to the Government, would make as able and formidable a body for their country's defence, as Great Britain, or Switzerland, or any Part of Europe, are able to produce.'

William Pitt the Elder started the process which eventually involved over fifty battalions of Highland troops who were raised to distinguish themselves in battle in places as far apart as Quebec, Seringapatam, and Waterloo. There was an astonishing metamorphosis in British perception as the so-called 'Jacobite traitors' of the 1745 Rebellion became imperialist heroes within twenty years. They carried their clan loyalties to their leaders into battle with them, and this made them politically trustworthy. Fraser's Highlanders (the 71st Highlanders) had six clan chiefs among its officers. The warriors who had repulsed the Romans were now 'devils in skirts' defending the Empire abroad. Many men from the Strathspey area wore uniforms and served in foreign fields, in the Strathspey Tenables, the 97th Foot, and the Seaforth Highlanders. In the uncertainties of Highland life and Highland harvests, at least there was a square meal a day in the Army – 'L'arme marche sur le ventre', as Napoleon is supposed to have said.

To most country folk, religion had seemed to be a constant in the vortex of current affairs. There was general superficial observance of religion by church attendance by at least half of the population. There was the repetitive round of 'hatches, matches and dispatches' – births, weddings and funerals. Funerals provided the best regular breaks in routine, with the whisky flowing freely and the exciting aftermath of a drunken brawl occasionally.

Peter Grant painted a bleak picture in his 'Sketch of My Own Life and Times', written shortly before his death. He wrote: 'the people of the Highlands of Scotland have been fearfully neglected regarding the state of their souls. The whole area was divided into parishes, some of them 60 miles long interspersed with mountains and lakes. Men under the name of ministers were placed in the parishes, but as there were no records and little communication, if any of these ministers knew the grace of God in truth, they were so few and far between that they made little impression upon the manners of the people. The people in general knew nothing of religion but to hear sermons, sit at the sacrament once a year, and get their children baptized, nor did they know in general that there was any religion in the world but their own. The people were strongly attached to the Gaelic language, but no Gaelic books were to be found, as the people did not know the value of learning. Although there were schools in every parish, many of the people were either not able or willing to send their children to school, and those who were sent were only taught to read English; not a word of which they would understand.

'As might be expected, the people were rude in the extreme, given to superstition, terrified at the signs of the heavens, spent much of their time Sabbath and week-day telling stories about Fairies, Bockies (hobgoblins), Loregoes, etc, by which children and others were terrified out of their senses; at marriages and christenings drinking dancing, shooting, swearing, and every lewdness was common; at funerals drunkenness and fighting was so common that one would cast up to the other, 'there was no fighting at your father's funeral'.

On 1 June 1881, Rev William Grant, third son of Peter Grant of the Songs, and third pastor of the Grantown church, wrote a brief account of the origins of the church, 'to supply as far as possible the want of a regular Church Book, and copied from the old church books by James Duncan, Pastor.' The following account summarises William's record of events.

The basis behind the disturbance of the status quo in the Strathspey area was an increasing groundswell of dissatisfaction with the preaching of the Establishment churches generally. The outward ripples of difference spread from an independent group which formed in Rothiemurchus.

The sound-waves of change and challenge in religious affairs emanated from Edinburgh, and from two brothers, Robert and James Haldane.

The Haldane brothers were people of wealth and property, who had colourful careers. They had become converts to Jesus Christ, and later became Baptist believers by conviction and immersion. Their work helped to give a new impetus to the growth of Independent churches in Scotland.

Robert Haldane (1764-1842) was born in London. He made the sea his career at first, but later settled in the family estate at Airthrey, Stirlingshire, which he inherited on his parents' unexpected death. He was converted in 1795, when he said: 'Christianity is everything or nothing. If it be true, it warrants and commands every sacrifice to promote its influence.' Robert sold land on his family estate, and poured money into Christian enterprises. The East India Company blocked Robert's plans to start a mission in Bengal, India, and he spent his time and money in mission elsewhere, establishing a seminary in Edinburgh with sixty students, for whom he undertook the cost of fees and maintenance. He funded the building of congregational tabernacles in Scotland, engaged in positive evangelism in Geneva, and was at the heart of spiritual revival in French-speaking Switzerland. JD Douglas said of him: 'A man of irenic and gracious disposition, he could be unyielding when he felt truth was in jeopardy…as with his brother James, his social standing opened doors of opportunity, yet his preaching was so simple and direct that it reached the hearts of all kinds of people.'

James Haldane (1768-1851) was born in Dundee. His parents both died before he was six years old. He studied at Edinburgh University, then joined the navy in 1785, and became captain of an East Indiaman. He resigned his commission, and after his conversion in 1794, he helped to establish the Society for Propagating the Gospel at Home in 1797. James, in the company of John Campbell went on the first of a series of preaching tours that covered most of Scotland. Haldane visited Grantown for the first time in the spring of 1805. It was market day, and a fair was in progress in the town square.

The place was crowded, not only with country people on business, but with a large contingent of troops stationed in the town. Haldane and Campbell chose a spot some two or three hundred yards from the square, and both preached. Before long, the fair was almost deserted, and a crowd gathered around the preachers. At first, some were inclined to laugh, but Haldane's voice, which had made itself heard in ocean storms, dominated the scene, and his message made an obvious impact on his hearers. An intriguing little scene developed. Haldane had little Gaelic, and he tried to draw into conversation two young people who had only a smattering of English. When words failed, Haldane used sign language, and Peter Grant and Ann Macintosh never forgot the experience, or the message. Apparently the Macintosh family had already had some contact with James Haldane, who had recently persuaded Ann's father to start the first Sunday School in Strathspey. (Robert Raikes, Editor of the Gloucester Journal, founded Sunday Schools in 1782, and reported 250,000 Sunday School children by 1784). James Haldane aimed to train preachers to evangelise throughout Scotland.

John Ferguson was one of these preachers. He was denominationally an Independent, and had been involved in a revival movement in Breadalbane in 1801. He was now engaged in a preaching tour of the North of Scotland, and arrived in Grantown in 1803. His message was a call back to the basics of the Protestant Reformation – the necessity of an experience of God's grace alone through faith alone, by the Scriptures alone, coupled with the sense of spiritual assurance, without winning any merit with God through human efforts. He made a deep impression on his hearers. Some forty years later, Peter Grant wrote: 'His doctrine was new, and fell like thunder on men's consciences.' Crowds gathered, listening in wonder, the news spread, and some felt prompted to travel up to sixty miles further north in search of an evangelical minister in communion seasons.

A local farmer named MacShimidh (Gaelic, English name 'Fraser') was among those stirred in spirit by Ferguson's message. Concentrating on the themes of sin and divine judgement, he began to preach most earnestly around the area. He had a powerful voice and an uncultured manner, but his call to flee from the wrath to come must have made him seem like a latter John the Baptist. He attracted a good following, including William Macintosh, whose daughter was to marry Peter Grant in 1806. In typical Haldane style, MacShimidh preached powerfully in the open air, and in churchyards as congregations were leaving after service. As winter approached, better accommodation was needed, and the local people built a turf meeting-house near the River Spey at Tullochgorum.

The parish minister had at first watched these developments with interest, but this was followed by growing concern, and William Grant told later how the meeting-house was burned down at the minister's instigation. News of this event spread rapidly, and MacShimidh was summoned to Edinburgh, where he was persuaded to remain within the Church of Scotland. No more was heard of him in Strathspey. Haldane's Society for Propagating the Gospel at Home sent more preachers into the area.

One of these preachers, John Reid, settled there for a while and was instrumental in the formation of the Rothiemurchus Independent Church in 1805, with a membership of about 30. John Reid built on the foundation of Macemie's message of divine judgement, by preaching a message of full and free salvation. Most meetings were held in houses or barns.

The newly-formed church at Rothiemurchus soon ran into difficulties of distance and geography. The members came from opposite ends of the district – from Grantown and Kingussie neighbourhoods. The arrival of two preachers fresh from Haldane's training courses, gave the opportunity to make a change. The membership divided and two new churches were set up – Kingussie, led by William Hutcheson, and Grantown led by Lachlan Macintosh.

Lachlan Macintosh became a significant figure in evangelical work in

Scotland. A native of Badenoch, he was in Perth in 1803, and visited the Tabernacle to hear James Haldane preaching. Haldane was beginning another tour, and used as his text 'Go and proclaim these words unto the north, and say, Return, thou backsliding Israel, saith the Lord; and I will not cause my anger to fall upon you: for I am merciful, saith the Lord, and I will not keep anger for ever.'(Jeremiah 3 verses 12-13).

Lachlan Macintosh was stirred in his spirit, and obtained an interview with Haldane, who easily persuaded him to undertake advance publicity for the preaching tour, as far north as Logierait.

The visit left Macintosh absolutely convinced that he needed salvation in Jesus, that no one could earn that salvation, and that the righteousness of Christ was a free gift of grace to every believer. Haldane's closing word to him when they parted was: 'Cleave to the Lord with purpose of heart.' Lachlan Macintosh had been converted, born again by the Spirit of God, and the basis for evangelism had been laid. Soon afterwards he was enrolled in one of the Haldane classes arranged in Edinburgh for training preachers.

The courses lasted for two years, and at the end of that time, with Haldane's financial support, Lachlan Macintosh returned to the North as an agent of the Society for Propagating the Gospel at Home. John Reid appears to have moved to Oban in 1805, and Lachlan Macintosh, the local man, seems to have undertaken the pastoral work as his successor at Rothiemurchus, where he presided at Communion services.

As already mentioned, the little church divided soon afterwards, and this left him free to concentrate his efforts in the Grantown area, where he became known as 'The Missionary'. Lachlan Macintosh had no patronage from laird or church, so initially he was regarded as a heretic, and his meetings were denounced as unlawful conventicles. The Laird of Grant was abroad at the time, but had left instructions forbidding Macintosh to preach in any building in the estate, and the people (his tenants) were ordered not to harbour him in their homes. He and his small but growing gathering of followers were mercilessly persecuted, and the naughty local boys disturbed their worship and abused the preacher. Duncan Dunbar's mother sympathised with Lachlan Macintosh in the treatment he was having, and warned Duncan to desist, saying: 'This is a man of God, my son. Be very careful how you treat him.' Services were held initially in private homes or in the woods, and the congregation grew in numbers. Lachlan Macintosh preached in the gravel pit outside of town, and eventually hundreds came to hear. Meanwhile he continued his study of the Bible.

Early in 1808, Lachlan Macintosh had to face a doctrinal issue. As an Independent preacher he was asked to baptize an infant, the child of a church member. He responded: 'Really, you must teach me how to do it. I see no precept or example for it, and do not know how in the world to do it.' Challenged on the matter, he denied the validity of infant baptism, and the issue was referred to James Haldane. In response to Haldane's request, Macintosh walked to Edinburgh, fully expecting that Haldane would produce evidence to prove that he had misunderstood the situation.

In fact, the reverse happened and, after thorough study, discussion and prayer, first Macintosh and shortly afterwards, the Haldanes were baptized by immersion as believers. Thereafter, Haldane's spiritual and financial resources were used to spread the Gospel according to Baptist principles.

Robert became a champion of evangelical Calvinism in Scotland and France.

On his return to Grantown, Macintosh offered his resignation as pastor, but after careful discussion the little church declined to accept it. Instead, they accepted the doctrine of believer's baptism, and were baptized in the River Spey. Seven were then formed into Grantown Baptist Church at a meeting held in Alexander Grant's house at Angach, near the old Spey Bridge.

The fledgling church had to face two obstacles – first, to gain acceptance in the local community, where the factor of the Seafield Estates was openly hostile, and second, to overcome the financial pressures on their pastor.

The first seems to have been gradually accomplished. Threats of eviction if any tenant invited Macintosh to conduct a service in a house in Grantown appear not to have been carried out, although it is probably significant that the Grant family at Angach moved house to Achnafairn at an early stage in the church's life.

Certainly, the pastor managed to obtain his own house in Grantown – a necessary arrangement for a married man raising a family. Eventually, their six children, and the cost of living in wartime, and immediately afterwards brought problems. The allowance granted by the Haldanes was only about forty pounds a year, so the pastor supplemented his income by part-time teaching.

The financial position probably improved in 1820 when one of Haldane's training courses for preachers was set up at Grantown. However, the financial pressures would not go away, and as a result Macintosh left Grantown for Dundee in 1826. From 1829 to 1832, he was pastor of Orangefield Baptist Church in Greenock, but returned to the North, serving for the next twenty years as the Travelling Agent for the Baptist Home Missionary Society for Scotland. In this way his ministry covered the whole of the Highlands and Islands, and his fund-raising activities took him all over Britain. Macintosh made a tremendous contribution as an itinerant preacher. He walked great distances to meet his commitments, and preached wherever he stopped for any length of time. On 4 June 1818, he sent a report to James Haldane about one tour which lasted from 15 April until the middle of May. He visited Cullen, Boyndie, Aberchirder, Banff, Portsoy, Whitehills, Balmaud, Fraserburgh, Inverallochy and St Combs. He was surprised to discover a cottage meeting in Banff, where several of the ladies took an active part, and he remarked: 'I must say for the sisters that their words were few, scriptural and to the point, but very few attended.'

Lachlan Macintosh had served the Lord faithfully at Grantown. The little church of seven members in 1808 now numbered 74, with a good number of additional attenders. He left no church minute book. John Fisher has suggested he was 'too busy making history to have time to record it.'

Now came another problem – how to find a pastor. Instinctively, they looked to the South, but a man who had fairly recently finished his training under Lachlan Macintosh had been planted by God among them. His name was Peter Grant.

CHAPTER FIVE –
FARMER, FIDDLER – AND NOW
FOLLOWER

The visits of Haldane's preachers to the Strathspey area gave Peter Grant a troubled conscience. Their message brought an itch he had to scratch. He was not happy with his lot as the local farmer and fiddler. The precentor at the parish church left to join Lachlan Macintosh's new church, and Peter had been appointed in his place, but this brought no satisfaction.

His personal crisis erupted when he attended a young man's funeral, and had an engagement to be the fiddler at a dance the same evening. He never played at that dance, nor at any other, and the parish church had an unhappy precentor on the following Sunday. The worship seemed utterly lifeless. He said to himself 'This will not do', and went out from the service and walked straight to Grantown to seek out the persecuted Baptists, and a more authentic spiritual atmosphere. He had to hunt for them, because every door in Grantown was closed to them by order of the Estates office. Eventually, he heard a Psalm being sung, and he found the group 'in a barren field near the village'.

What had been happening to him? The theological term used to be 'conviction of sin'. In the earlier section of his little master-piece 'The Christian's Great Interest', written around 1658, William Guthrie had set out the unusual ways that God calls people to Himself. Some were called from the womb, and some were graciously called at the hour of death, like the thief on the cross, but the book majors on 'God's more ordinary way of calling sinners', down the well-trodden path of an increasing sense of sinfulness and need for God, then into repentance and being enabled to exercise a God-given faith in the finished work of salvation accomplished by the sacrifice of Christ once-for-all on the Cross, and culminating in the new birth, and the assurance and joy which is the birth-right of every true believer.

On that night in the barren field, with that despised little group of worshippers, Peter found peace with God, and responded with the frequently-quoted words of Psalm 132, verse 14 (metrical version): 'This is my rest, here I'll stay, for I do like it well.'

Events moved rapidly for him. In 1806 his father died, and Peter took possession of the farm at Ballentua. Soon afterwards he married Ann McIntosh, daughter of the founder of the first Sunday School in Strathspey. Their marriage was a very happy one until she died 28 years later, leaving eight children.

However busy he was in the ensuing years, Peter carved out time for meditation and study in the Word of God. In later years an officer who heard him preach was so impressed that he asked him where he received his theological education. Peter replied : 'Between the stilts (support handles) of the plough.' Some might have said it with a hint of bitterness or deprivation. Peter could say it with a twinkle in his eye.

Extracting a living from the land was a difficult task in those days. The topography of the area meant that hill-farms had somehow to be made fertile; the plough had to go up many a barren hillside, and much of the best land lay water-logged and unused.

GM Trevelyan says 'the primeval forest had disappeared, and as yet no modern plantations, hedges or walls broke the monotony of the windswept landscape, where the miserable sheep and cattle shivered in the blast. Although the Union of Parliaments in 1707 had opened England's markets at home or overseas for the Scots, the Highlanders were fighting for the very existence of their own folk, in subsistence farming.

Wresting a living from the land was 'a sair fecht'. (a sore fight).

We are not sure how advanced the Agricultural Revolution was in Strathspey, but Peter Grant lived through some radical changes in farming methods.

The old systems meant that arable farming was carried on in open fields. Sheep and cattle were able to rough graze on hills, moors and bogs, and this land was known as the common. This right was important to a rural economy. The nature of ploughing under old systems meant that reclaimed land was farmed in long narrow strips. Lack of winter feed in the earlier period meant that there was a massive slaughter of livestock, and a tragic loss of good breeding stock. Soil would not support repeated grain harvests, in the absence of artificial fertilisers. Consequently, eighteenth century farmers had to leave a field fallow, or idle, every two or three years.

Open field farming was gradually eroded by the system of enclosures. Farmers gathered their strips into consolidated holdings, which were then withdrawn from the open field system. The limitations of open field farming were obvious. It was inflexible, and new crops were hard to introduce. It wasted time because farmers had to travel to work different strips. It favoured the lazy, whose weed-producing land blighted neighbouring strips. It prevented selective breeding to improve the quality of livestock. It wasted crop production by the proportion of fallow land lying idle each year. Landowners seeking what they called 'improvements' brought large numbers of the tough West Highland strain of Black-faced sheep into Strathspey.

There were tremendous pressures for change because of rapid population growth, and hungry mouths to feed. Rising prices forced farmers to follow the more efficient system of enclosures. The pressures were intensified because of the long War period from 1793-1815, which prevented imports and made improved farming methods essential.
The new farming techniques included the Norfolk system of four-course rotation of turnips/barley/clover/ and wheat, which eliminated the fallow year. Lord ('Turnip') Townsend headed this movement.

'The Honourable Society of the Improvers of Agriculture in Scotland' was formed in 1723.

Lord Kames attempted to spread the gospel of his farming experiences on his farm at Blair Drummond by 1776. James Small of Dalkeith introduced an improved plough. James Meikle and his son Andrew introduced better methods of winnowing and dressing grain.

An Act of Parliament appointed a team of surveyors and commissioners to ensure fair distribution of land. Enclosure was expensive, and landowners had to pay up to 25 shillings an acre for surveyors and commissioners fees.

There were significant improvements in Scottish agricultural production

during Peter Grant's lifetime. The yield of oats went up 200 - 300% between 1750 and 1800.
Meat output also increased six-fold from the 1750s until the 1820s.

There was a thorough transformation of the landscape, with enclosure sweeping through the Scottish countryside, and older rigs or ridges of land being replaced by hedges, ditches or dry-stane dykes.

Tenant farmers' rents rose a lot during the Napoleonic Wars, although the Wars brought some prosperity. The period from 1815 until about 1830 meant higher rents and lower prices. The 1815 Corn Law prohibited the import of wheat when British wheat prices were below eighty shillings a quarter. By the 1830s, British agriculture slowly emerged from the recent acute recession.

In Scotland great strides were made in drainage techniques, largely through the lead taken by James Smith of Perthshire from the 1820s. By the 1840s, clay field-drainage pipes were available in large quantities. By 1847, machines were capable of producing 20,000 feet of pipe daily.

Spreading lime and manure increased, which helped to improve crops.

Large-scale use of artificial manures progressed, and bone dust began to be used as fertiliser. By the mid-1840s, over a quarter of a million tons of Peruvian guano was being imported to Britain annually. There was also an acceleration of the use of sown grasses and the use of turnip husbandry, although this came more slowly.

New machinery and the use of steam power in threshing and even ploughing helped farm production in the 1830s and 40s. The seed drill was at last coming into general use in this period. The biggest expansion in farming lay in dairying, and output of milk, butter and cheese increased. Enclosed farms, and selective breeding techniques along the lines set out by Bakewell about a century earlier bore fruit at last. By the 1830s Scotland's agriculture was producing models for others to follow, especially in the fertile soil of East Lothian, where they were using phraseology like 'factories for making corn and meat.'

Progress was helped in Scotland by the relative absence of peasant land rights, which slowed the process of rural transformation in other parts of Europe. In Scotland, multiple tenancies could be more easily reduced.

We are not sure how much of all this was adopted by Highland farmers, but it was one of the major periods of change Peter Grant lived through.

A close relationship developed between the young farmer Peter and the Baptist pastor Lachlan Macintosh, who recognised that the young man had talents that could be encouraged and enhanced.

The pastor challenged Peter to see which of them could produce the better Gaelic poem in the style of Dugald Buchanan within one week.

Peter won the 'contest' and was encouraged by this to compose several more poems. Friends urged him to get them published and so in 1809 the first edition of his 'Spiritual Songs' appeared. The book was a great success, and was reprinted on several occasions.

Dain Spioradail became so popular as a Gaelic hymnbook, that, when people emigrated to the far-flung frontiers, they took the little book with them.

The poems met some unfriendly criticism. 'The Men' were a distinctive class of teacher-leader-evangelists in Highland Presbyterianism. They were a powerful force in parish life, especially as interpreters and expositors of the distinction between godly and ungodly at communion seasons. This stern faction, who formed a spiritual nobility within the Church of Scotland, attacked his poem on a Young Child in Heaven, which gave full expression to a parent's deeply-felt love. As a result, some people stopped attending services Peter conducted; but the demand for the book continued.

Lachlan Macintosh encouraged Peter to preach as well as to compose poetry. Tours through what were termed 'the destitute parts' of the district had led to the establishing of a number of cottage meetings. Those attending were poor faithful folk living a number of miles from Grantown. Peter had a broad outlook, and preached in both Baptist and Congregational meetings. He was technically functioning as a lay missionary for some years until 1826. John Munro, Congregational minister at Knockando in Morayshire, gave his full support to Peter's ministry until some of his members began to talk about believers' baptism. He told Peter that he planned to write a pamphlet against this idea. Peter tried to dissuade him, but in 1825 the pamphlet appeared. Its title was: 'An Inquiry into the principal questions at issue between the Baptists and the Paedobaptists on the subjects and mode of Baptism.' We have Peter's response in his own words in his 'Sketch of the Origin and Progress of the Baptist Church in Grantown', which he wrote from Ballentua on 20th June 1854:

'In the year 1825, an Independent minister in our neighbourhood published a book against the Baptists, particularly against our church. As the drift of the book was an attempt to prove that the church of God was the same in every age, and grounded his arguments on the covenants made with Abraham and the nation of Israel, it was highly extolled by the ministers of the national church, who recommended it to their congregations, as they clearly saw it was much more favourable to national churches than to Dissenters of any kind; but it opened the mouths of many against us. Mr McIntosh thought it best to let the book alone. I thought otherwise, but I knew I was far from qualified to write anything for being published; but as I had a little leisure from my farm in a stormy winter, I thought I would try how the book could be answered, and wrote a manuscript, defending our character and principles. Being on a tour next summer, my wife and family began to show the manuscript -rather as a curiosity- till at last it came into the hands of Mr McDonald of Aberdeen, and other friends, who thought it should be published, to which I made no objection, if they thought it might be useful. So in due time, (1827) it appeared; and whether what took place afterward may be ascribed less or more to the book or not, the result was, that the Baptists continued to prosper; and since the Independent minister published his book, his flourishing church began to decline, and is now nearly extinct, if not wholly so – the few remaining likely to go back to where the book was leading them.' Peter felt strongly about the issues, but he did not enjoy public controversy.

Early in the 1820s, Peter had joined one of the Haldane courses for preachers. Lachlan Macintosh ran the course in Grantown. It was attractive and convenient, but time-consuming for the young farmer.

His wife pleaded with him about his late-night study. His children begged him to lie in bed a little longer in the mornings (he was regularly about his work at 6am). He told them: 'I must be up and in the field with you by six o'clock. It would never do for the ungodly to say that it was all very well for Peter Grant to go preaching and praying at night, when he can be in his bed in the mornings.'

In 1826, Lachlan Macintosh had to face up to his problem of limited income with a large family to feed, and gave up the pastorate at Grantown to leave for the South. Shortly afterwards, the church invited Peter Grant to fill the vacancy.

The young Peter Grant

Peter, an experienced lay preacher, and trained as a home missionary, was in his early forties, and considered the matter carefully. He felt it was a pivotal moment in his Christian life, and not one for a hasty decision.

The church could offer no financial support, and he would have to continue to work at Ballentua, After discussion, the church agreed that he could practise open Communion, although some members did not like it. All candidates for membership would have to be baptized by immersion unless a situation arose where the whole church decided to make an exception. On the strength of these agreements he accepted the invitation.

On 30 June 1829, he was ordained and set apart for the work of ministry following the laying on of hands by William Hutcheson (Kingussie), William Tulloch (Blair Atholl), James Millar (Rannoch), and John McPherson (Lawers).

The induction service at Grantown may also have ratified Peter's position as an agent of the Baptist Home Mission. Around this time, he took a house in Grantown, and left the management of the farm at Ballentua to his son Peter, so that there must have been some improvement in his financial position. He soon reorganised the Grantown house to become a place of worship as well as his home, helped by friends in Aberdeen, and a local Excise officer. This arrangement illustrates how things had changed since Lachlan Macintosh's time. The icing on the cake was that Peter lived in his house rent-free for many years!

Peter had experienced the reality of the Lord's word to Samuel in
1 Samuel 2 verse 30: 'Those that honour me I will honour'.
He had honoured God in the matter of his call to Christian ministry,
and the Lord ratified it in his family life and Christian service.

CHAPTER SIX –
'ITINERATING EXERTIONS'

Events in England helped to shape the responses of evangelicals in Scotland in the later eighteenth and early nineteenth centuries. Two Anglican clergymen who became open-air preachers, George Whitefield and John Wesley, were at the forefront of the Evangelical Revival in the mid-eighteenth century. This was the last Revival to affect broadly the whole range of British society. Both men came preaching to Scotland, with varying responses. Whitefield visited Scotland fourteen times, particularly during the revivals at Cambuslang and Kilsyth. At Cambuslang in 1742, his preaching to huge crowds was used by God to give a second wave of revival there. Wesley's Arminian theology, with its stress on human choice rather than God's sovereignty in the matter of salvation, did not go down well in a country strongly influenced by the Calvinism of John Knox and the Westminster Confession.

The broad river of activity in Highland Baptist life was fed by at least three tributaries in the early eighteenth centuries.

The first was the efforts of the brothers Robert and James Haldane, mentioned earlier. The Haldanes provided the financial launch of the Society for Preaching the Gospel at Home (SPGH) in 1798. They funded itinerating evangelists in the Highlands, spent significant sums producing Bibles and religious tracts, and helped to fund buildings where 'The Haldane Preachers' could be heard. Unfortunately, in the controversy which followed their conversion to the Baptist cause in 1808, the SPGH collapsed. The Baptist Highland Mission was founded in 1816 largely through the work of William Tulloch of Blair Atholl. It was a minor attempt to compensate for the failure of SPGH. The Haldanes became embroiled in various theological controversies, and some of their activities in the Highlands were regarded as politically subversive. They actually spent around £70,000 on Gospel work between 1798 and 1810. The work in the West Highlands and the Hebrides was pioneered by Dugald Sinclair, who reported of evangelical work and church-planting in six volumes entitled 'Journal of the Itinerating Exertions in Some of the Most Destitute Parts of Scotland'. He was supported by Christopher Anderson from Edinburgh, rather than the Haldanes. On a preaching trip, Dugald Sinclair preached to the invalids at the spa in Strathpeffer, and met up with Christopher Anderson in the market square at Beauly.

They travelled together to Inverness, and preached simultaneously on opposite sides of the river, each with about 1500 hearers! Then they travelled south by coach.

Professor Donald Meek comments: 'The itinerants were essentially field-preachers who conducted their services wherever willing audiences could be found. Cottages, barns, tents and schoolhouses provided shelter initially, and continued to be used where there were no church buildings.'

The second tributary was the missionary aftermath of the Evangelical Revival. Andrew Fuller, a Particular Baptist pastor from Kettering in Northamptonshire shook the nest in his book 'The Gospel Worthy of All Acceptation' (1785). This book stirred up missional activity at home and abroad. William Carey, a Baptist shoe-repairer and teacher from Northamptonshire, produced a famous treatise, 'An Enquiry into the Obligations of Christians to use Means for the Conversion of the Heathens in 1792, and the Baptist Missionary

Baptismal site, River Spey, seen from Old Spey Bridge

Society (BMS) was formed in the same year. William Carey set sail for India in 1793. Andrew Fuller visited Scotland five times, and reached Aberdeen and Dingwall. News of the Baptist Mission to Serampore filtered through to Strathspey, and widened the horizons of Peter Grant and many other Baptist Christians.

The third tributary was the Baptist Home Missionary Society for Scotland (BHMS), founded in 1827, which built on the earlier work initiated by the Haldanes. The Society worked mainly in rural areas of northern and western Scotland, although there were a few stations in the south of Scotland. The work of the Baptist Highland Mission was subsumed into BHMS in 1827. BHMS was well organised, and employed agents to raise funds for the support of itinerating evangelists, including men like Sinclair Thomson in Shetland, William Fraser, Christopher Anderson, - and Peter Grant. By 1844,there were twenty-eight evangelists. Lachlan Macintosh became the first travelling agent for BHMS in 1831. He worked in Scotland, and won good financial support from English Christians. These itinerant missionaries made valuable contributions to evangelical efforts, and BHMS produced annual reports, detailing their work. Peter Grant was an experienced and well-travelled preacher by 1826, when he accepted the invitation to become pastor of the Grantown church.

Professor David Bebbington points out that there was a significant spurt in the number of Scottish Baptist churches founded between 1800 and 1810. Twenty-three out of forty-one churches were founded in the period 1808-1810.

I will include Peter Grant's comments in his reports to BHMS relating to revival in a separate chapter, but his other comments indicate how busy he was, and how busy and needy the area was, in evangelical terms.

We set the scene with descriptions from BHMS preachers in the 1837 Report.
'When on my tour, those who formerly very kindly invited me to their houses, would scarcely speak to me, owing to their distress from lack of victuals... crossed a high mountain to --------. Hungry, wet and wearied, under wind and rain, we were directed from one farm to another, till we reached the head of the glen, before we could get lodgings....Arrived at --------------; but

as there was no inn or public house in the glen, we found some difficulty in procuring lodgings, although at every house we promised to be content with whatever they gave us, and to pay them for their trouble…. Their poverty thins our meetings, and also those of the Established Church, for seldom can a person appear decently clothed, without borrowed articles; so that the fitting out of one impedes two or three….the measles and fever are keeping pace with one another, often meeting in the same family…..in many instances within my own knowledge, the heads of families can give nothing to support nature, except an unripe potato much damaged by the frost. They have not, nor can they obtain upon credit what would make a drink of gruel for their little ones; so that where God does not put it into the heart of a friend or neighbour to pity them, their case is most wretched.'

The approach of the 'Hungry Forties' was matched by a heart-hunger in the hearts of God's people for a spiritual break-through. The following is an extract from a preacher's letter: 'An affliction has come over this country like a cloud….many poor people are in great want of bread, and will be still more so. Trials must be expected; the Gospel is despised, and who can escape who neglects so great salvation. There cannot be a greater sin than unbelief, and it is sad to observe its prevalence, connected with the love of dress and vanity of mind. A great judgement, or a great mercy, is at hand, for the Lord will have His people gathered out of the world. Oh, what a loud call is there for all the Lord's people to assemble together, and to cry mightily to Him to pour down the Spirit from on high, that the churches may be revived, and sinners awakened, and that the glory of the Lord may shine forth! I trust we have beeen praying and waiting, and we shall not wait in vain. The Lord says: 'Ye shall seek me and find me, when ye shall search for me with all your heart.' O glorious promise! May we have faith to rest upon it.'

Trawling through the reports submitted by Peter Grant for Home Mission, we gather that he engaged in itinerant preaching two evenings a week. He did a summer preaching tour with William Hutcheson from 30th June until 23rd July, 1829 in Glenurquhart, Beauly and Fortrose, and in 1831, reaching Strathnairn, Lochend, Abriachan, Drumnadrochit, Strathglass, Kilmorack, Beauly, Strathpeffer, Dingwall, Evanton, Fortrose, Rosemarkie, Nairn and Dulsie. He toured again with William Hutcheson in 1832 to Strathdearn, Laggan, Strathnairn, Aberarder, Stratherech, Fort Augustus, Glenurquhart, Beauly, Kiltarlity and Loch Ness. He comments on the problem of distant members (as far as 60 miles away!), and outreach Sunday schools as far as 15 miles away.

He notes in his 1830 report an improvement in the spiritual quality of parish ministers, and in education with good consequences for Gospel preaching. His preaching tour in 1833 was a stamina-sapping effort to Laggan, Fort William, Stratherrick, Lochend, Dochgarroch, Abriachan, Milton, Lochletter, Glenconvinth, Strathglass, Beauly, Strathpeffer, Strathearn, Barra, and Dores.

There were no long tours in 1834 because of his wife's illness, and in 1836 because of serious illness. His wife died in 1837. In 1838 he visited Badenoch, and Strathspey and Badenoch in 1839.

Add to all these itinerating exertions his pastoral work and Sunday preaching (at least twice) at Grantown, his farming activities, midweek prayer and Bible study meetings, and family responsibilities, and you have a workload that would kill a horse! Yet here he is, reporting on Grantown in the BHMS report for 1839:

'June – We have still to praise the Lord for His goodness. As a church we have our trials, like all churches in the wilderness, but, on the whole, we are united in love, heart, and hand, in the work of the Lord. For the last month, our meetings have been well attended; several are asking the way to Zion, with their faces thitherward; three have been baptized lately; the number baptized during the past year, fifteen; may their names be written in the book of life! Our stations in the country are well attended, and better supplied than ever, as some of the young men preach in the places which I cannot attend. We now have eight Sabbath schools in different parts of the country, from which we hope the Lord will have a seed to serve Him when we are laid in the dust.'

CHAPTER 7 –
FAMILY MATTERS

A helpful way to deal with the details of Peter Grant's dealings with his family is to hear it 'from the horse's mouth'. He wrote what he calls 'A Kind of Memorandum book – a Statement concerning our own Family.' This document illustrates the honesty, generosity, and integrity of the man in his practical relationships with his family.

'I Peter Grant was born January 30th 1783.
Married to Ann McIntosh in 1808, both about 23 years. My wife died January 2nd 1836 of dropsy (fluid collection or oedema, probably due to heart or kidney malfunction –GJM) which continued 4 years…but she lived and died in the faith.
James Grant – our son was born November 30, 1810.
Isabella - our oldest daughter was born March 20, 1813
Ann Grant - our second daughter was born May 14, 1815.
Peter Grant- our second son born September 5, 1817.

The family, Ballintua Farmhouse

Janet Grant - our third daughter born September 20, 1819
William Grant – our third son born August 1, 1823
Margaret Grant – our fourth daughter born June 6, 1825
Christina Grant our fifth daughter born August 1, 1828

I myself married a second time to Janet (affectionately known as Jessie) Grant – July 9, 1852, myself aged 69 and she aged 31 years, married by Mr Ferris, Minister of Edinkellie.

October 6, 1853 brought us another period of our life. We have on that day received a man child from the Lord, and desire and pray that he may be devoted to the Lord who gave him, even from his mother's womb.

His name is Donald Haldane Grant.

6 March 1857. The Lord gave us cause again to rejoice and to bless the Lord who gave us a young daughter on that day, whom we call Annabella Grant – for we pray and hope that she may be the Lord's in that day when He makes up His jewels.

In another statement entitled 'WORLDLY AFFAIRS OF OUR FAMILY', he sets out the way in which he had fulfilled his obligations to the eight children of his first marriage before tying the knot once more.

'John Grant Topperfettly married to Isabella Grant 3 March 1839. Isabella received from her father a £1 at Martinmas 1839. Again she received £10, besides a feather bed which is all she can claim of her father's property as she early left the family and did not work so much for the family as her sisters.

James Grant, merchant, Grantown, Deacon of the Church married Elsie Shaw 28 March 1839. This James our oldest son received at the time of his marriage £30 besides food and fuel for sometime; received £2 more in the year 1839 besides the rights of my house in Grantown was given over to him in 1852 on the condition that I should possess of the one room of the same house as long as I live so that he has no right to claim anything more belonging to his father.

Peter our second son married 1849. The toun and covering of the same (i.e. the farmtown of Ballentua – GJM) was given over to him by his father and by the consent of his children on the terms and conditions stated in another document so that he has no more claim on his father's property.

Peter Grant Auchnafearn married to Ann Grant our second daughter sometime in the year 1835. Got a cow worth £5 at her marriage, and £1 in the year 1839 and £5 on 12th September 1850 and £2 on 13 June 1852. Ann received £2 October 1852, which makes £10 besides the cow which is all she is to receive of her father's property in all she can claim.

Jessie Grant our third daughter was married to Robert Grant- Broomhill January 12, 1850. Jessie received £10 the day of her marriage. Jessie also received £10 July 6, 1850, which is £20 in all as her share at least till the other daughters get as much.
Margaret Grant my fourth daughter was married to John Grant, Knockambuie March 15, 1850. Margaret received £10 October 16, 1851 as a part of the £20 promised her at her marriage. Margaret also received £1 June 12, 1852, and £3 afterwards.
Christina Grant my youngest daughter was married to John Jackson of Glasgow on 15 June 1852 by her father and at her father's house the share of her father's property was twenty pound sterling, of which she got £10 in her hands a few days before her marriage. £5 was paid for her expenses. She gifted the other £5 to her father. The other £10 she distributed among her sisters. Again she received £10, besides a feather bed which is all she can claim of her father's property as she early left the family and did not work so much for the family as her sisters.

It is probably suitable to break into father Peter's narrative to quote from one of his letters.

Peter, aged 69, was married for the second time, to Janet (or Jessie) Grant, aged 31, on 9 July 1852.

In a letter from Ballentua dated 12 July 1852, here is the 69-year-old newly-wed dad writing to his 24 year-old daughter and her husband: 'my dear Christina and John Jackson, Dear children, Grace mercy and peace be with you. You know a little now of married life, and it rejoices my heart to know that you are happy together and that you can walk together as heirs of the grace of life, and truly if my prayer or blessing would have any influence to make you comfortable for time and eternity you deserved them and you have them. And I believe Christina, that your kindness, and your affection to your father is now returning to yourself in an affectionate husband. And now since the Lord has been so gracious to you, let your chief concern be to glorify Him with your bodies and spirits and remember always that you are bought with a price and that you are not your own, that in all things you will give yourselves first to the Lord and then to His people according to the will of God, holding fast the profession of your faith, without wavering, and if you thus honour the Lord, He will honour you, bless you, and make you a blessing. I believed from the beginning that your union was of the Lord, may it be also for the Lord, and to the Lord, so shall you be lovely in your lives, and have an abundant entrance into the everlasting kingdom of our Lord and Saviour Jesus Christ.

I received your kind letter, and would have written to you long ago were it not my own unsettled state, but now what I have purposed long ago, and which I believed to be my path of duty, is now over in a quaint manner which I hope will do no harm to anyone. Yesterday was the first Sabbath (since his marriage – GJM) and it passed over very agreeably, I preached twice myself, and William preached once, and in the interval as many as our room could contain gathered in, and we had a few happy hours together. Those who were much grieved have not got it altogether out of their minds yet, but to all appearances, a few days will wear it off. Blessed be the Lord. As to my own happiness, you will say it is too soon yet to judge, but so far as we have gone, my most sanguine hopes are realised....I got a most affectionate creature, whose whole concern is to make me comfortable. I would not touch upon these things, were it not that I know you to be anxious to hear about them....

Always happy to hear from you, though I do not wish to press you knowing that you must correspond with many. Praying always for you, I remain dear children,
Your affectionate Father, Peter Grant.

Peter Grant, Ballentua, married Mary Grant November 1849. Peter Grant had his first-born son August 28, 1850. Peter got possession of the toun and all the covering of the same in the year 1848 on the conditions mentioned in another document.

William Grant my son has been lawfully married to Ann Grant his cousin, December 12, 1850. William is to receive for his share of his father's house more of the expenses of preparing him for the ministry, besides he is to get £25 which falls to his father's share of Margaret Stuart's money only this will not come to William's hands till the death of Margaret Stuart, (probably one of his mother's Ballinluig relatives).

Jessie Grant my third daughter was married to Robert Grant January 12, 1850. Jessie received £10 on the day of her marriage and also £10 on July 6 1850, which completes her share of her father's property.

Margaret Grant my fourth daughter was married to John Grant, Knockambuie March 15, 1851. Margaret received £10 October 16, 1851 and £7 June 12, 1852. Margaret my daughter or her husband received £2 December 16, 1852. Margaret my daughter or her husband received £1 in March , 1853, which completes the £20 promised to her at her marriage, and is all she can claim of whatever belonged to her father.'

Changes were taking place in Peter's household. His wife Ann had died on 2 January 1836, and Peter the widower had brought up the eight children in addition to carrying out his pastoral and preaching duties. No doubt the older children shared the load of running the household. When the last of his children left home or got married, Peter was left on his own at the age of 69. He writes about things in 1852. 'All my children had married, and were comfortably settled, and I was left entirely alone, and having some years before, formed an attachment to a young woman, whose name was Janet Grant, (also known as Annie and Jessie – GJM), daughter of Donald Grant, Shanval, much younger than myself, but in every other respect I saw none so suitable, in her piety I had the greatest confidence, and her attachment to me was beyond doubt, after having often sought direction from the Lord, we have come to the conclusion that it was our duty to be married, and so we joined hands, 9 July 1852. Although all might see that her chief object was my comfort, yet she suffered much opposition, both from my people and her own. Some were against me also for marrying at my time of life a second time, and some were afraid that it might give offence and hinder my usefulness. Others were afraid that we could not live upon such a small income, having never exceeded £40 a year, but I have got one from the Lord who is truly a helpmate, who can live like myself, having depended all my days upon what the Lord would send....The cause is prospering, souls are converted, additions are made to the church, and we are happy together as our hearts could wish...'

He surprised the congregation and community by announcing his engagement. This would of course set the tongues in the district clacking, partly because of the great difference in their ages, and partly on speculation about how they would manage on Peter's modest income. It must have been quite a shock to the system for the family to get their heads round the idea that their step-mother was younger than some of them! Adverse comments soon subsided, and they were left in peace, as everyone could see that a very happy marriage had begun. Peter and Janet had two further children, Donald Haldane Grant in 1854 and Christiana, making a neat total of ten!

Peter's letters to his family reveal a deep spirituality in his longings for them, an intimacy and warmth towards them which is salutary, and a time commitment to them despite the demands made on him. I major on his letters to Christina, the youngest daughter of his first marriage, and William, his third son, who partnered Peter in ministry, and eventually succeeded him as pastor in Grantown.

There are also a few additions by Peter Grant Junior.

Here are some examples:

11 November 1851: 'My dear Christina, May the Shepherd of Israel watch over you night and day when separated from your lowly but sweet home, and from the lovely and sweet family circle in which you have moved and acted your part to the delight of your dear Father in days and years that are past. I would have written oftener, but reflecting on what is past, and that the future is a mystery, I am over-powered, and I will have to stop – but why did I say that the future is a mystery? God is His own interpreter, and He will make it plain, far far beyond the starry skies we shall all meet as a family in heaven of which according to the course of nature, your Father will be the forerunner; blessed hope, and blessed Saviour on whom our hope is built,

and blessed Spirit that hath shed the love of God in our heart, so that our hope will not make us ashamed.

Cleave unto the Lord, and grieve not His Spirit; He and He alone can comfort, guide and strengthen you. Make Him now the guide of your youth, and He will smooth your way, soothe your spirit, and sweeten your every enjoyment of life. 'His love in time past forbids me to think He would leave you at last in trouble to sink…'

27 January, 1851: 'My dear child, May heaven bless you, and make you a blessing. I early thought that the Lord had something remarkable to do for you, and by you, and I think providence and grace are developing it more and more every day, and I have no doubt that His grace will be sufficient for you in all the varied scenes through which you may have to go, commit your way unto the Lord, set Him before you in all things, and He will stand at your right hand so that neither life or death nor things present nor things to come shall be able to separate you from the love of Christ.'

18 March 1852: My dear Christina, Your worldly path hath yet been like the morning light; may your spiritual path be the same, shining more and more until the perfect day so shall your peace be as a river, and your righteousness as the waves of the sea; trials you may expect, but be of good cheer said Christ, I have overcome the world. I know you were well aware from the beginning that the higher you rise in the world your trials would not be less; so I do not think you aspired after it, but in following the leadings of providence, you may expect the Lord to be with you, to guide and help you to the end and though all our life would be trials, they are not worthy to be compared to the glory that shall follow…'

22 March, 1852: 'My dear Christina, The Lord will be your guide, Christ will be your portion, Angels will be your guard, and the Holy Spirit will lead you into the land of uprightness. Were it not that my days are near a close, I do not know how I could bear the thought of you being so far separated from our family circle, but the thought that we would not be long together here whatever, reconciled me to that mysterious providence which separated you so far from the friends and companions of your youth, and brought you to act a part, and to move in a higher circle, for which it doth not appear that you had any ambition, and since it is the doing of the Lord, it becomes us

all to adore His name, and pray that He may enable you to answer your calling, and serve your generation according to the will of God. Joseph was far separated from his brethren, and Esther was brought to share a throne, to bring about the great purposes of the purposes of the most high. It is our consolation that he who is to be the companion of your joys and sorrows is one whom Jesus loves, who will be careful that your soul may be bound in the bundle of life, and with whom you can take sweet counsel going to the house of God, and who will not necessarily draw you to places or companies but where Christ and His disciples will be.'

Christian families have to work to make a living.

It seems as if Peter Grant Junior became more of a key player in running the farm as his father's pastoral responsibilities increased.

A few extracts from letters from his father to William, along with postscripts thereto from other family members, give added insight to this. William at this time would have been in Fortrose studying with Mr Shearer, the Baptist pastor there.

The extracts reveal family affection and concerns, and practical matters regarding farming in the Strathspey weather.

Extract from an addition to a letter from Peter Grant Senior, 28 February 1844:
'We cannot do anything out of doors just now. I chiefly work in the new house. Jess will tell you all that I have been doing. (Jess is the third daughter Janet born last before William).

The mare is not well yet.

I would write to you every day if I could get time. I would send you plenty papers if I thought you would get time to read them. I bought a leg of pork to send to you.
Yours truly, Peter Grant, Junior.'

Addition by Peter Grant Junior to letter dated 26 April 1844:

'Dear William, I do not think that I need make any apology for not writing for a long time, for you know what I have to do; for I made three yokings every day since the storm went away, and if I ever was near baffled, it was this week. (yoking is harnessing horses for a spell of work) We will be ready for the potatoes the first of the week if all is well. We were taking home lime this morning. I think my Father's plan of your coming away on Monday will suit me, for I think that I can manage to have all the potatoes down by Saturday night, and the horse will be rested Tuesday for going away on Wednesday again, for I have little expectation that Jean can be put in the gig owing to her sore shoulder. She was not in the gig since you went away....You must write next week and state to me the day you are to come, the road you intend to come, and the place where I must meet you. The time I must be there. I may state to you that the monthly prayer meeting will be on that Monday night. I could not get the potatoes down as James sold his horse, and I think it now best now to delay till you come. You seem to be much afraid that you will have to speak; it is evident that you must speak, at least at the prayer meeting on Sabbath morning. You better prepare some sermons, and very long ones too! My time is done. Yours truly, Peter Grant, Congash.'
(Congash is the farm at the bottom of the road to Ballentua – GJM)

Letter from Peter Grant Senior, 20 August 1845.

'Our harvest will be very late, no sunshine, but constant rain for two weeks, but the Lord reigneth, let the earth be glad. May we wait for the Lord as they that watch for the morning, Na He will come to us as the former and latter rain. Love to dear Mr and Mrs Shearer, and all the friends, from your affectionate father, Peter Grant.'

Postscript to letter from Ballentua, dated 22 September 1845.

Our harvest is ready for the sickle, but the days are wet and exceedingly cold, potatoes spoiled with the frost, and some of the corn a little damaged, but a good deal remains if safely gathered in…

Postscript to letter, 11 June 1846.

'Dear William, We are exceedingly busy tonight, as it's the night before market, so I have no time to write you but a few lines to let you know we are thinking very very long, especially Sally. We have Mr Gilbart, just haste haste haste home, your sister Maggie.' (this is Margaret, fourth daughter of Peter Senior and next after William in the family).

Letter from Ballentua, Wednesday 24 June 1846.

' Dear William, I can only write you a few lines. We are all well, but we never had such a time with thunder, lightning, rain and hailstones, whole day. We had two feet of water in the house, everything in the barn was swimming, fanners overturned, flooring raised etc. The water made fearful gulfs between us and the moss. Several cattle were killed through the country, much crops spoiled, many if not most of the country bridges fell, but the bridge of Spey stood yet. Saturday and Sabbath were fine days. Monday night we had fearful thunder and lightning and another flood most of the night, yesterday toward evening thunder, and another flood continued all night and up to this hour no abatement.
Your father, sincerely, Peter Grant.'

Postscript to letter, 12 December 1846.

'My dear William, Having room I will add a few lines to let you know what I am doing. When the storm commenced about two weeks ago, I commenced to thrash the Bear (i.e. barley, GJM). I have three tracks of it done, delivered 8Qrs. To Mr McGregor at £1:10, making £12.. Being some more nor the rent. I have 2 Qrs. yet for meal, and one stack for sud and meal. And I have got two stacks of Oats thrashed. Making 7 Qrs. Of Oats which I have to make into meal, so that I have plenty of straw till the winter is over.

I had no difficulty getting one to thrash with me owing to the storm. I worked from 6am to eight at night every day of this and the last week excepting today. We had a dreadful day yesterday with blowing.

I got a very good coat like your gray one, two beautiful vests and a very fine pair of trousers and a pair of new shop stockings out of the parcel…. In haste, I remain yours truly, Peter Grant' . (junior).

(The letters have occasional references to cholera, which was prevalent at different times at epidemic level, a comma-shaped virus which comes from polluted drinking water, and because of the rate of dehydration can kill within a few hours. The fear of death it brings may have been a factor in people turning to God in the Strathspey area).

CHAPTER EIGHT–
PETER GRANT THE PREACHER

Before we begin to take a look at Peter Grant's preaching, we should consider what has been called a 'dying art' in an age of texting and sound-bytes, and a population conditioned by Mirror and Sun to what we call 'the tabloid mind' which demands brief, punchy news digests.

Preaching has been defined as 'truth conveyed through personality'. It has also been described tersely as 'an attempt to wake the (spiritually) dead in half an hour'. If poetry is 'logic set on fire', perhaps preaching could be called 'truth and conviction set on fire in speech'. The mind and emotions as well as the voice are involved. John Bunyan said: 'I preached what I did feel, what I smartingly did feel.' Some preachers have earned reputations for the sound of their voice, like John 'Chrysostom' the 'silver-tongued' preacher of

Grantown-on-Spey Baptist Church, built 1851, enlarged 1901

the fourth century, or George Whitefield, who could be heard in the open air by thirty thousand people without amplification, or Jock Troup who could be heard a mile away speaking in Bangor in Northern Ireland. George Whitefield was enthused in his speaking skills in the Bell Inn in Gloucester, listening to dramas being presented by professional actors in the establishment run by his mother. There is always a dramatic element in preaching. A preacher was once said to ask an actor to make a comparison between actors and preachers. The actor said, rather cynically, 'We speak fiction as if it were truth - you speak truth as if it were fiction!' Preaching is distinguishable from teaching or lecturing in that it has an inherent aim to challenge people into mental and spiritual response and decisive action. Jay Kesler would put the stress on the mental and spiritual side when he comments, 'We're not human doings, we're human beings.' Some preachers think modern life calls for abbreviated messages, to suit the tabloid mind . AW Tozer's comment was that 'sermonettes make Christianettes.'

The authority of the preacher lies outside of himself. He/she speaks to people as one who has spoken to God, so the Old Testament prophets can say: 'Thus says the LORD', or they preface their prophecies by saying 'Oracle of the LORD.' The Hebrew word translated 'oracle' in that phrase can have the onomatopoeic nuance of the murmured intimacies expressed around the camp-fire late at night. Preachers must preach, and prophets must prophesy. The eighth century BC prophet Amos has a section of inexorable 'cause-and-effect' events, which he climaxes with the statement: 'The lion has roared, who will not fear, the Sovereign Lord has spoken – who can but prophesy?' The eighth century BC prophet Micah writes: 'But as for me, I am filled with power, with the Spirit of the Lord, and with justice and might, to declare to Jacob his transgression, to Israel his sin.'

Jeremiah the prophet had such a hard time of it, he decided to keep quiet, but he discovered that the Lord's word was like a fire shut up in his bones, and he could not keep it in…'His word is in my heart like a fire, a fire shut up in my bones. I am weary of holding it in; indeed, I cannot.' (Jeremiah 20 verse 9)

On the issue of how the preacher moves from Biblical text to preached expression, Rev GB Duncan, a prince among preachers, gave (as those of us privileged to hear him would expect!) a three-fold guideline - Analyse the

Text, Crystallise the Truth, Humanise the Telling.

In defining the nature of preaching, John Stott highlights:

TWO CONVICTIONS ABOUT THE BIBLICAL TEXT.

1. It is an Inspired Text. 2. It is to some degree a closed text – it requires exposition and explanation.

TWO OBLIGATIONS IN EXPOUNDING THE TEXT.

1. Faithfulness to its Content. 2. Sensitivity to the Modern World.
Stott says: 'We are neither to falsify the Word in order to secure a phoney relevance, nor are we to ignore the modern world in order to obtain a phoney faithfulness. It is a combination of faithfulness and sensitivity that makes the authentic expositor.'
Stott refers to Dr Lloyd-Jones' comment in his book 'Preachers and Preaching' that the decadent eras of the church's history have always been those in which preaching has declined.

TWO EXPECTATIONS IN CONSEQUENCE.

We can expect God's own voice to be heard. 2. God's people will obey Him. We respond to God's voice by humbling ourselves before Him in worship, penitence and confession, and laying hold on the Saviour.

The preacher is a herald, or an apostle or a teacher, all of whom need external accreditation for the authority of their message. Peter Grant made the move from Gaelic to English as a teenager, and preserved his heart-felt expression in his Gaelic poems, but the record shows he was a more than competent word-smith in English, so that under God's authority he was able to speak the language of the heart to his hearers.

Theologically, Peter Grant was a strict or particular Baptist, whose preaching reflects what Donald Meek calls 'a warm-hearted evangelical Calvinism'. Calvinism had a strong influence in Scotland. It was imported there by John Knox from Calvin's adopted home in Geneva. John Calvin, or Jean Cauvin (1509-64) was a French theologian and reformer who escaped

France to avoid persecution, attempted to set up Geneva as a model Christian community, and wrote the most influential book (developed from a pamphlet) of the Protestant Reformation – 'The Institutes of the Christian Religion' (published in 1536). Calvin's views became enshrined in the Scots Confession of Faith (1540) and the First Book of Discipline (1560). The 'Five Points of Calvinism' can be summarised in a simple but helpful acrostic summary in the word TULIP. T = Total Depravity. Since Adam's Fall, human nature has been polluted with sin. We are not as bad as we can be, but there is no part of our human nature which is unaffected by sin, U = Unconditional Election. God has predestined some souls for election and salvation, by His sheer grace, with no basis whatsoever on our merit or worth. The reach of God's electing grace affects all without distinction rather than all without exception. L = Limited Atonement. The Lord Jesus Christ died for His elect, and His work of salvation is restricted to them. I = Irresistible Grace. The gracious work of the Holy Spirit in bringing people into an experience of salvation is an inexorable process. P = Perseverance of the Saints. Those who have been elected for salvation, and born again by the Holy Spirit, cannot fall from grace. They will persevere until they reach heaven. Some Christians are 'Four-and-a-Half Point Calvinists', in that they have reservations about accepting God's predestination to damnation, which they claim is the logical but not the Biblical teaching.

The extreme Calvinism of the Hyper-Calvinists made some believers unhappy with the free offer of the Gospel to sinners by preachers. They would agree with the parody to the hymn 'Rise up, O men of God', and would be happier with the parody: 'Sit down, O men of God, there's nothing you can do; God can achieve His purposes without the likes of you!' Andrew Fuller's book 'The Gospel Worthy of All Acceptation' (1785) attempted to prove that authentic Calvinism was essentially a missionary theology, and inspired new life in the Particular Baptists of Northamptonshire.. The original title of the Baptist Missionary Society was 'The Particular Baptist Mission for Propagating the Gospel among the Heathen'.

This was, broadly, the theology which sustained people like Andrew Melville and Samuel Rutherford, George Whitefield, Sandy Peden, William Carey, Jonathan Edwards, John Paton - and Peter Grant.

The contemporary expression of the Gospel seems somewhat removed from this theology. The rescue dimension of the Gospel is diluted, and it is unusual to hear people say they have been 'saved'. The stress is more on 'my commitment', or 'my spiritual journey', and saving faith is no longer qualitatively distinctive from faith in a coach driver when you step on his coach, or in an airline pilot when you step on his plane. Peter Grant's robust and warm-hearted Calvinism is a welcome break from the prevalent brash and self-confident church attitude which assumes that God must be fortunate to have me on His side!

In Peter Grant's preaching, the assumptions are consonant with a Calvinistic emphasis.

In the early 1820s, Peter joined one of the Haldane's courses for preachers, held in Grantown, and led by Lachlan Macintosh.

Lachlan Macintosh introduced Peter Grant to preaching, and initially Peter addressed cottage meetings which had been formed as a result of itinerant preachers on tour in what were called 'the destitute parts' of the area. Peter preached at both Baptist and Congregational meetings. The 'Sketch of the Life of The Rev Peter Grant', published in 1867, says 'He thought out his own subjects, but wrote only a few brief notes. He never published anything beyond the poems, except a book on the subject of Baptism, in answer to a little volume by a neighbouring minister, which answer was very successful, both as to argument, spirit, and result.'

'He would insist on family worship being held in his room, to the very last, and would join in the psalm of praise, and kneel at prayer'.

I have in my possession a ring binder containing about a hundred and eighty hand-written pages, notes of Peter Grant's sermons, most of them lovingly taken by George Fleming, the church clerk or secretary of Grantown-on-Spey Baptist Church, during the period January 1851 until October 1852, when Peter was 68 years old. The notes were kindly made available to John Fisher of Inverness by the Grant family. Some of the notes are more like extracts than full sermon scripts. This author had serious difficulties reading and transcribing the hand-writing!

I am very grateful to Terry L. Wilder, who reproduced edited extracts under the title 'The Lost Sermons of Scottish Baptist Peter Grant' (Borderstone Press, 2010). I was also comforted to read that Dr Wilder received assistance from Michael McMullen and several of his church history students in transcribing the sermons! (Dr McMullan was pastor of Harestanes Baptist Church, Kirkintilloch, Scotland, where I was also pastor for six years).

We can write authentically about Peter Grant's preaching because of a thick notebook which came through one of his descendants, Mrs Margaret Cumming, in Grantown. Peter Grant was usually the preacher at every service –his son William is not mentioned. Readers can make their own comparisons and contrasts with modern approaches in ministry.

The texts show a steady progression in some detail through Matthew's Gospel at morning services, taking a year to proceed from chapter 12 verse 26 to chapter 16 verse 29. Evening sermons covered a wide range of topics from Old and New Testaments – prophets, Psalms, Epistles and Gospels. The only visiting preachers recorded are Rev George Tulloch from Ross-shire, and a Mr Douglas. In later years, Brownlow North and Grant of Arndilly were regular visiting preachers.

Although William Grant was later to refer to frequent Communion services, the notebook shows them only twice a year, in April and October, on the Presbyterian model. On these occasions, there were special texts (John 5 verse 24. 1 John 1 verse 7. Malachi chapter 3). Communion services were very serious occasions. For example, on 6 April 1851, Peter set out his message under these headings:

The hopeless state of 'those who do not hear Christ', What is to be understood by hearing and believing, and The privileges of the believer.

After a brief pause, he proceeded to 'fence the tables', that is to protect the Lord's Table from any profane or superstitious use, specifying who were not to partake of the bread and wine – unbelievers, nominal Christians, those with unchanged lives, all who normally neglected the means of grace, swearers, Sabbath-breakers, and 'all who violate the law of God in life or conversation.' He followed that with the detailed invitation to participate to 'all who have heard and know the name of Christ, all who felt their need of Christ, all who needed quickening in their souls, and those who saw themselves as 'poor, hungry sinners'. Such Communion services seem serious affairs when compared to the perfunctory 'add-ons' we sometimes experience in today's churches.

In a sermon dated April 12, 1851, on Matthew 13 verses 10-18, Peter Grant says: 'The man who comes to the Lord's Table unworthily – instead of doing him good, it really seals his judgement and makes him more sinful….Men are represented here as being afraid to hear the Word of God, afraid to be converted willingly. They shut their hearts with other concerns, afraid of being brought back to God, afraid of being brought into a state of holiness. They are shut up to the truth because to be converted is to allow that we are condemned under the curse of God. It is not easy to admit all this. We will try rather to meet the favour of God by works of our own doing, afraid of being converted. We are afraid of being healed, so we count disease an honour. No, no; we will rather try and conceal it. People are afraid lest the Spirit of God makes them to see that they are spiritually diseased.'

On Communion Sabbath, April 6 1851, Grant preached on John 5 verse 24: 'Verily, verily I say unto you, he that heareth my word, and believeth on Him that sent me, hath everlasting life, and shall not come into condemnation; but is passed from death unto life.' The preacher explains some of the nuts and bolts of salvation.

He asked the question 'What are we to understand by hearing God's Word and believing on Him that sent Him? It implies something more than a mere rational hearing. Thousands hear Him so. It is hearing the awakening Word of Christ. It was His awakening voice that made Paul fall down on his way to Damascus. It was this voice that awakened the 3000 on the Day of Pentecost….mere awakening does not confer everlasting life. The substance of hearing the Word of Christ is coming to Him for salvation. Receiving Him is having life. Before we receive Christ we must be living souls. Power is then given to receive the Son of God. The righteousness he then received in being made alive from the dead, he then believes and receives Christ, and has everlasting life…. It is conferred by being disconnected with the first Adam. If no mind could describe the curse of breaking of this covenant, no more can they describe the blessedness of recovering it from the second Adam. This everlasting life implies full enjoyment of God, nearness to God, the presence of God; he has access to God. It is this that is worthy of the name life. Second, he shall not come under condemnation. Because of the absolute perfection of Christ, he shall never fall under it again. He is brought to judgement, true, but the object is to be justified before men and angels. Third, the stability of his condition is that he has passed from death into life….He is transferred from the state Adam was in after the Fall to the state he was in before the Fall. He has this life by union with the second Adam….These are high privileges indeed, but they are not greater than him who purchased them. Let us not be surprised that the obedience of Christ secured them. Consider Him on Calvary, bearing the sins of His people in His own body on the tree and you may indeed wonder at the free grace of Christ in conferring them on such vile sinners as we. But again consider for whose sake they are conferred, and you will cease to wonder.'

In his sermon on Matthew 15 verse13 following, Peter Grant says: 'Every doctrine in a church not planted by Christ shall be rooted out…Every scribe, Pharisee, priest, minister, elder and deacon not planted by God shall be rooted out – every such man that has attainment to some office in the church by false keys, by the false keys of graceless communicants giving calls to graceless men to offices in the church…..Coming to the Lord's Table, and eating the children's bread, only imagine a dog coming and taking of the bread and elements of the children of God. You would be horrified at the sight. So remember that the children's bread will not convert the unconverted, uncircumcised dogs. God knows their heart and soul.'

On June 8, 1851, Peter Grant preached from Matthew 13 verses 33-36, where the Lord Jesus said: 'The kingdom of heaven is like unto leaven, which a woman took, and hid in three measures of meal, till the whole was leavened.' The preacher said: 'The New Testament church shall one day cover the earth as Abraham's seed covered all Canaan….the people of God are the salt and life of the world. The world would have been destroyed ere now by its own corruptions were it not for the church of God…we are not to understand (the leaven – GJM) as if Christ was afraid Satan would find out He had a kingdom in this world. He tells Satan and all this world in secret I have done nothing and my church shall cover the whole world. …it is a mark of the true church that she is employed in converting the world around… a (fine) saving grace of God makes very little noise. You will not hear the leaven making a noise. It is true conversion. It is not done in a storm. You never see the work going on, but it endureth forever, uniting (people) to the grace of God…it was a historical fact that the children of Israel were fed by the manna. It was more than a parable. It was an illustration of Christ, the Bread of Life. All these facts were intended to illustrate the Word of God. They could not understand the people coming out of Egypt as people converted….It was a secret that the Gospel must be preached to every creature, secret on account of the few who understood it….that is our concern, to make them understand that we are witnesses for the truth. If we are the people of God, we will employ every means to extend the Gospel.'

Other special services recorded in 1851 include a Fast Day on Wednesday 8 October, and the Thanksgiving Day on the first Sunday in December. Harvest comes late in the Highlands, and this seems to have been the Harvest Thanksgiving with appropriate sermons morning and afternoon.

The notebook of sermons presents an intriguing puzzle. The handwriting and spelling suggest that it was written in haste, but if the notes were taken during the service, how could this be done without attracting attention before the age of fountain pens or biros?

Peter Grant had very limited written resources at Grantown, especially in the earlier years. Here is part of a letter written by Mr N McNeil to Mr Spence in Edinburgh dated 15th November 1820:

…. 'I made some enquiry with respect to his (Mr Grant's) library – it is very small indeed. He has neither a commentary, nor a dictionary, except a small English one. Were a few necessary and well-chosen books procured for him, it might be of great service for the improvement of his mind; and such is his thirst for information, that books I believe would be more acceptable than money. I have no doubt but there are hundreds of Christians in Edinburgh, who have great numbers of useful volumes lying in their libraries covered over with dust, which might be put with advantage into the hands of Mr Grant and his like.'

Those desirous of contributing to assist Mr Grant in his disinterested labours, or wishing further information respecting him, may apply to:

Charles Spence, Writer, in Edinburgh;
Mr John Munro, Inverness;
Mr William Matthews, Aberdeen;
Or to any of the following Ministers of the Gospel:
Mr Neil McNeil, Elgin.
Mr James Dewar, Nairn.
Mr John Munro, Knockando
Mr Neil McKechnie, Inverness.'

Peter Grant's preaching is thoroughly Biblical. Every sermon is based on a Biblical text or theme. The level of Scriptural references given throughout his sermons is high enough to indicate that the preacher may have had limited resources, but is 'a man of the Word', with a mind saturated in Scripture. A spot check on one sermon yielded 31 direct biblical quotations, and several Biblical allusions.

Peter Grant had a lovely view of the intimacy between God the Father and the Lord Jesus Christ His Son. Preaching on a Fast Day the week before Communion (October 8, 1851) he commented on John 1 verse 18, 'the only begotten Son, who is in the bosom of the Father': ' Christ was wrapped and closed up in God's love at the Last Supper. The disciple Christ loved leaned on His bosom, but Christ was different. He was embosomed in the Father's bosom. I was an only son whom my father loved. I lay in his bosom, rejoicing always before him. Parents, think of an only son, and you have a faint idea of my love to my dear son. The persons delighted in each other. The Father and Son rejoiced together; the holy Father and the holy Son rejoiced together…there was a glorious union between these two persons. And He, in His memorable prayer in John 17 asks that they may be one as they are. The distinction of persons is 'I and my Father'. It is not one in will and design; it is one in nature. Nothing in heaven or earth can give but a faint idea. It is only creature love, one or two instances. Jacob to Joseph, all his sons and daughters rose to comfort him and he refused to be comforted, and to Benjamin Judah said, when he was a prisoner in Egypt, my father's life is bound up in the child's life; if you kill him, you kill my father. Jonathan and David : their souls were knit up in each other. These are Bible instances, but it is a shadow only of the Father and the Son's love.'

Peter Grant preached of the reasons for Christ's sacrifice. On October 12,

1851 he preached on John 10 verse 11: 'I am the good shepherd: the good shepherd giveth his life for the sheep'. 'He laid down His life most willingly and cordially. It was not forced from Him by His Father, or by the prince of the air, the god of this world....He laid it down unreservedly. He laid it down to be be at the disposal of God's justice and wrath....No doubt God loved His people with an everlasting love. And loved them so much that He gave His Son for them, but there is a higher end by Christ laying down His life than the salvation of His church. The glory of God and the manifestation of His grace was a far greater end that the salvation of His people....If we were only guided by the Spirit to Calvary and the cross to see such sighs, groans, and tears! We were in a low condition from the height we were in. We are become so low that there is between us and the lowest hell a connection, and unless that connection is broken, of necessity we must go to the lowest hell. We were guilty of breaking faith with God, of breaking covenant with God, guilty of high treason of trying to dethrone God.'

Commenting on Matthew 15 verses 21 forwards, Grant says:

'He (the Lord Jesus Christ) seemed to illustrate here that He would have a people from among the Gentiles...He knew what means to take to bring her from among the Gentiles. She came alone; we are not told any came with her. There is something noble here to see a poor female coming such a journey alone to profess Christ. If ever we come to Christ, it must be alone, single, not as a congregation...Her appeal went to His heart, (see) the tenderness of Christ to the poor and needy... She could not come near Christ for a multitude of dead professors. There are always numbers of dead sinners in the way of poor souls coming to Christ...How trying for a mother to see her daughter made to do the work of Satan in the hands of Satan... Mothers, don't fight with your daughters. Mothers, scold less and pray more. They would succeed better. This poor soul is an example.'

'He was in His personal ministry not to exceed the land of Judea, neither His disciples till after His ascension, but whether He was sent to Jews or Gentiles He never before put the question whether they were Jews or Gentiles. We know He came to save elect sinners....In His personal ministry indeed He was only sent but to the house of Israel, but in reality He came to save His church... (This woman) said; 'Truth, Lord, I am an unclean dog.' She was satisfied to receive a crumb. He gave her a full answer, 'O woman, great is thy faith', putting the people of Israel to shame. You see the benefit of persevering. She obtained the desire of her heart. Satan was that instant disposed. She obtained such a healing that made her willing to be spent for Him...'

In the afternoon of 14 December 1851, Peter the Preacher made his position clear when he was preaching on the nature of saving faith from Luke 7 verse 50: 'thy faith hath saved thee': He quoted from Hebrews 12: 'Christ is the Author and Finisher of our faith', and from Ephesians 2: 'By grace are ye saved through faith, and that not of yourselves.' Mr Grant said: 'We are to be saved through no merit of our own....True repentance of sin is essential to salvation, but never is a man saved by repentance. Did He (our Redeemer) say 'thy repentance hath saved thee?' No, 'thy faith hath saved thee.'

Saving faith is not human. It is not in us; it is the grace of God. Before we obtained it we were guilty, dead, a mass of corruption, a mass of confusion, without one good principle. Is it possible that such a faith could come out of such a mass? We are infinitely guilty and exposed to misery....You would as soon expect it out of the belly of a bottomless pit as you could expect it from such a heart of wickedness....Where are the servants of Satan that smell and declare that damnable doctrine that we can take possession of Christ when we please?....It is a divine principle, a power God gives of His free will to a sinner that is killed by the law. We are as much dependent on God's free will to bestow it upon us as we were for the gift of His own Son.'

Peter Grant used illustrations in his preaching. Illustrations are to a sermon what windows are to a building. The very word 'illustration' means 'enlightenment.' Some preachers produce 'buildings with no windows', and others produce a 'veritable Crystal Palace' of a sermon. I was privileged to hear the preaching of Dr D.Martyn Lloyd-Jones. He rarely used illustrations from contemporary life, but frequently used Old Testament illustrations to back up spiritual truths. He probably used this approach to teach the Old Testament to his congregation.

Peter Grant used illustrations from his context as a countryman, a farmer and a Highlander. These were very well chosen. He was once gently chiding his folk for their preoccupation with discussion on predestination and election. I will quote the description given by John R Thomson in a lecture delivered in Kilbride Parish Hall, Isle of Arran, on 3 March 1903, referring to Peter Grant's treatment of Luke chapter 13 verses 23-24, 'Are there few that be saved?...strive to enter in at the strait gate...' Mr Thomson said 'He began with a twinkle in his eye and a broad smile on his face: 'I'll tell you what some of you are like, my friends. You all know I have a small farm, and a few cows....you know how it is the practice before putting in the cows for the midday milking, to give them an hour or so in clover, or at least in the better grass than their ordinary pasture. As it drew near the hour for them to get to the clover, they all drew towards the entrance gate to it. When I opened the gate, they all rushed in, and all, with the exception of one poor foolish brute, eagerly set to work, feeding at the hardest, showing distinctly that they knew their time was limited, and were determined to make the most of it.

'The one foolish brute that I have mentioned had scarcely passed through the gate, when her eye fell on an old shoe. She picked it up, and began to chew it, as some foolish cattle will do, you know. Well, I endeavoured all I could to make her drop that shoe. I chased her round and round the park till I got fairly exhausted, but utterly failed to make her drop it. I sat down, and allowed her to have her own way. For the whole hour, while the others were busy feeding and satisfying their appetites, this poor silly brute chewed and slavered at that worthless old shoe, her mouth and breast covered all over with froth...this poor brute went home nearly as empty as when she came out in the morning.

'I saw several of the noisiest opponents turn red in the face, and wince visibly. They had an idea of what was coming.

Pausing for a moment, looking at the audience keenly in the face, and pointing the finger at them, he solemnly said: 'That's like you, my friends. There's a Gospel feast spread before you in the Bible; plenty nourishing food there. That won't satisfy you, however. If there is any knotty point from beginning to end of it, you must fix on that, like the silly cow on the old shoe. At present you have got hold of the old shoe of Election, and you have been chewing it, and slavering over it for a year or two. The danger is that you will chew and slaver till death overtakes you. Take warning in time, then, and cease prying into what does not concern you. Strive to enter in at the strait gate...'

As the work at Grantown-on-Spey developed, Peter had up to fifteen preaching 'stations' outwith Grantown, and his day would often stretch from six o'clock in the morning in the fields until midnight, returning home from preaching. Sometimes he spent half the night writing out thoughts produced in the course of the day.

Sometimes he went on preaching trips for several days, and the hospitality was not exactly Ritz standard. He discovered when he was staying the night in one crofter's cottage that the livestock went in the same door as the humans at night (presumably to keep them warm, and prevent theft). The crofter had kindly laid out some fresh straw in the corner for the visiting preacher to sleep on. Peter was awakened in the middle of the night by the horns of a cow...he said it was quite disturbing to be wakened up by an animal trying to eat your bed! On another occasion, he confided in a letter to his daughter that he had misjudged the depth of the snowfall, and set out on his journey home after a preaching trip to Drumuillie, aged 69! He exhausted himself travelling through three feet of snow, afraid to leave the road, and unable to see any houses which could provide shelter. He left early in the morning, and reached Curr (3 miles SW of Grantown, and 5 miles from Ballintua) by 'the gloaming' (dusk). This was in January 1852.

Sometimes, Peter Grant's sermons reveal his poetical, mystical nature, and the reader is transported, and faced with very direct language.....Preaching on Hosea 14 verse 5, 'I will be as the dew unto Israel', he says: 'Every night in the land of Canaan there was a very heavy dew causing the very land to rejoice. As the rose and the lily, most fitly did this represent the people of God. Christ, their Beloved, descends by the power of grace into their hearts. First, the calmness with which it descends. The Israel of God are not aware of the descent, but they feel the dew of God's grace. He does not say, 'I will descend in a thunderstorm.' That is a different work. The dew enters into the very stem of the plant so the grace of God has a most penetrating influence. Second, the sanctifying grace of God. It comes into hidden parts of the heart and beautifies His own Israel. Nothing produces growth like the dew. Their spiritual growth depends on this dew. Whatever scorchings, failings and weatherings they may sustain, the descent of the dew will awaken up all. Their soul is restored again to its beauty and comeliness. The effects are that they shall grow as the lily. Nothing is so refreshing to the soul as the grace of God.

Withering and death must be the result of those to whom the dew does not descend. They are dead in trespasses and sins. The Word of God has no effect upon them. Eternal death will soon be the result! Note the watchfulness and care of God. I will descend as the dew. The poor broken-hearted shall come in for their share. See the inexhaustibleness of this grace. It is as fountains of living water; it flows as free as ever. God's Spirit is not straitened. All fullness dwells in Him. For those who do not receive this dew a time will come when they shall be where a drop of cold water shall be denied to them – to be eternally in flames and to remember the plenty there was and to spare there! They despised it and set it at nought.'

Lord Handyside heard Peter Grant preaching once, and said to his friend, Robert Bruce of Kennet, father of Lord Balfour of Burleigh,

'That is a born preacher', and his friend replied, 'His sermons are poetry.'

ONE-SENTENCE GEMS FROM THE SERMONS.

God has not given us words to speak as we like for vain conversation or foolish talking.

Christ is precious only to those who found they were lost.

Satan can do more harm with one hypocrite than with a score of infidels.

If you do not have Christ, why eat and drink damnation?

The Lord's Table does not give life; it only sustains the living.

Jesus went from the Table to the Cross; we should not be at the Table unless we have been to the Cross.

The saints of the Old Testament period were redeemed on His credit.

The spiritual presence of Christ is in His ordinances, Him seeing them and them not seeing Him.

Lay hold of Him by faith, and men, angels or devils cannot deprive you. The Establishment is not the Church.

Had Christ not taken human nature, He would not have had a church.

All the heresies and enmities occur while men sleep.

One of Satan's victories is when he gets in a graceless minister.

We become partakers of His suffering as our souls rise in holiness.

David felt the comfort of the covenant when he fell under the chastisement of his father.

We have time enough; if not, that would bring a charge of injustice against God.

If parents have not the grace of God, God often allows the children to dishonour them.

You cannot serve God twice dead – under the law and under the power of sin.

Mothers, don't fight with your daughters – scold less and pray more.

God the Father loves Christ for what He is in Himself, and loves believers for what they are in Christ.

Don't depend on your enjoyment or comforts; Christ is your true consolation.

Trace in your minds, and don't say the God of Israel is your God unless you desire to meet Him.

The people of God need to have their eyes and ears opened and their taste refined.

We see the love of God in electing His people and the love of Christ in redeeming them.

God never gave thirst to the drunkard nor hunger to the glutton.

Private thanksgiving to God is not enough – it must be public.

Thanksgiving is a breathing of gratitude to the Person who paid the price we cannot pay.

Grantown Baptist Church, interior

CHAPTER 9 –
REVIVAL DEFINED

Throughout the middle years of the nineteenth century, membership of the Grantown church increased steadily, with occasional bursts of growth and activity which can only be explained as God's revival blessing. With help from Aberdeen, Peter Grant adapted a house in Grantown as a place of worship. He preached around six times a week, including twice or three times on Sundays. He was ordained on 30 June 1829. Donald Meek reports by 1833, the premises had to be enlarged. In 1848-49, there were so many enquirers that every member of the church was engaged in counselling new converts, and the church became one of the biggest Baptist churches in Scotland, with responsibility for seven Sunday Schools outwith Grantown.

'Revival' is an over-worked and misused word, so our first task is to discuss the meaning of the word, to look at its main criteria, and then to bring the events at Grantown under scrutiny.

Since the verb 'to vivify' means 'to enliven, to animate, to give life to' the term 'revival' must mean 'to restore life, to re-animate', that is, to repeat the procedure of giving life. One of the prayers frequently used in connection with revival is 'Do it again, Lord!' Martyn-Lloyd-Jones catches the flavour when he writes:

'It is an experience in the life of the Church when the Holy Spirit does an unusual work. He does that work primarily amongst the members of the Church; it is the reviving of the believers. You cannot revive something that has never had life, so revival, by definition, is first of all an enlivening and quickening and awakening of lethargic, sleeping, and almost moribund church members.

'Suddenly, the power of the Spirit comes upon them, and they are brought into a new and more profound awareness of the truths they had previously held intellectually, and perhaps at a deeper level too. They are humbled, they are convicted of sin…. and then they come to see the great salvation of God in all its glory, and to feel its power.

Then as a result of their quickening they begin to pray. New power comes into the preaching of ministers, and the result is that large numbers of people who were previously outside the Church are converted and brought in.'

William Fleming defines revival as 'Divine visitation'. It happens when God bursts in on the Christian scene. It can come as unheralded as a thunderstorm. Rev Duncan Campbell, who was deeply involved in the Lewis Revival, defines it as 'a community saturated with God.' He also commented: 'When revival happens, you do not need to have a publicity campaign. God does His own advertising.'

Skevington-Wood writes that revival rekindles 'the passion for souls', and includes the following features:

- an intensified awareness of God
- jealous concern for truth
- an absorbing concentration on prayer
- an exciting realisation of (evangelical) unity

Stephen Olford, whose expository ministry has been exercised mainly in America, distinguishes 'revival with a small r' from 'Revival with a capital R'. 'Small 'r' revival refers to personal or localised revival. 'Capital R' Revival refers to a thoroughgoing work of God which alters communities.

To emphasise the need for preparation for Revival, Stephen Olford uses the imagery of a becalmed sailing-ship (the church in its un-revived state) and the responsibility of the sailors on board to set the sails so that they are ready when the wind comes.

Charles Finney believed that God was bound to react by granting revival if the conditions He set were fulfilled by His people. The majority view represented by Jonathan Edwards regards Revival as entirely a work of God rather than a work of man. Revival is a largely unheralded, uncontrived eruption of God's presence and power among His people. This results in a significant, large-scale disturbance of their present state, a deepening of their spirituality, and a partially measurable, long-term impact of the Gospel upon the surrounding community of unbelievers. To take a later example, in the 1859 Revival in Ulster, public houses and racecourses suffered a drastic reduction in business, and a spectacular long-term drop in the crime figures. Revivals occur within the evangelical communities of believers, and there is often an individual or a small group of individuals at the heart of the action. The Old Testament narrative relating to the dedication of the Temple in the time of Solomon (2 Chronicles chapter 7 verse 1 following) helpfully highlights some features of God's intervention in revival: 'When Solomon finished praying, fire came down from heaven and consumed the burnt offering and sacrifices, and the glory of the Lord filled the Temple.'

The four elements here are:

1.PRAYER. Most revivals are born in prayer. George Whitefield said in the eighteenth century 'our Saviour loves to let us see greater things.' John Livingstone spent the whole night in an agony of prayer at Kirk O' Shotts before 21 June 1630, when over 500 people came to Christ. The hearts of John and Charles Wesley and their friends 'were strangely warmed' as they prayed at Aldersgate on 24 May 1738. There were ten prayer groups active every Saturday when revival erupted during John Balfour's ministry. There were 39 weekly prayer meetings going on connected with St Peter's church, Dundee when God broke through during the ministry of Robert Murray McCheyne. John Turner of Peterhead, a diminutive dying man riddled with tuberculosis, with a dreadful squint and a feeble voice, was at the heart of a prayer movement in the 1859-60 revival in Aberdeen. In the Welsh Revival 1904-05, there were about 40,000 people in earnest prayer in the Penarth area.

At Grantown-on-Spey, Peter Grant's leadership dampened down the spectacular elements often witnessed in revival. He was sensitive to any elements which would exalt the glory of man in competition with the glory of God. He examined new converts carefully, and refused to hold any special 'revival meetings', preferring to foster the regular prayer gatherings of the church, with occasional times of fasting as a sign of dedication to God. The church had two regular times of prayer, which were intensified during waves of special blessing, with a palpable sense of the Lord's presence, and over two hundred attending the midweek prayer meetings. Prayer was paramount in the Grantown church calendar.

2. FIRE. 'Fire came down from heaven'. Revivals come down. Fire burns

up the dross. This can be true literally in the lives of God's people in revival. The Ndani people turned to God in great numbers in the Swart Valley of Irian Jaya, Indonesia in the 1950s, and had a huge bonfire of their idols and fetishes. Fire sensitises, and one of the valid signs of revival is heightened awareness of sin, which often brings a desire to make restitution. During the spiritual wave of blessing in Belfast in the 1930s and 40s, large numbers of shipyard workers came to Christ, and Harland and Wolff's shipyards had to build sheds to hold the considerable quantities of stolen goods returned by workmen!

Fire purifies, and there has always been a cauterising effect as part of God's revival blessing.

Fire spreads in revival, and areas surrounding the epicentre are affected. The miles seem to melt away, and perspectives of time, distance, personal comfort and decorum are altered. In Jonathan Edwards' New England, as part of the aftermath of his sermon on 'Sinners in the hands of an angry God' on 17 July 1741, many people in the surrounding area were affected. It was reckoned that the spread of the revival from about 1734 onwards affected about 50,000 out of a population of about 250,000.

3. POSSESSION. 'fire consumed the burnt offering and the sacrifices.' In the Old Testament sacrificial system, the total burnt offering was consumed by fire. The apostle Paul uses the imagery of the burnt offering in his appeal to Christians in Romans 12 verse 1: 'Therefore I urge you, brothers, in view of God's mercy, to offer you bodies as living sacrifices...'

Sometimes the central figures in revival are acutely aware that they are possessed by God. Jonathan Edwards wrote after his conversion in 1720: 'there came into my soul, as it were, diffused through it, the sense of the glory of the Divine Being, a new sense quite different from anything I had experienced before. From about that time, I began to have new ideas of Christ...and the glorious way of salvation by Him. And my mind was greatly engaged to spend my time reading and meditating on Christ, on the beauty and excellence of His person....the sense I had of divine things would often, of a sudden, kindle up, as it were, a sweet burning in my heart, an ardour of soul that I know not how to express.'

1. GLORY. 'and the glory of the Lord filled the temple.' The Hebrew language has two kinds of verbs – active and stative.

Stative verbs express a state, or condition. The Hebrew Old Testament word for 'glory' comes from a stative verb which means 'to be heavy'. It expresses the state of a king weighed down with his kingly robes and riches, like crown and sceptre.

It is a manifestation of God in His sovereign power, and is often associated with overwhelming light phenomena and fire. (see Exodus 16v10, 24v16, 40v34. Isaiah 6v3. Ezekiel 1v28, 43v2-4,5. Hab 2v14). This iridescent shining sometimes produces an eruption of joy and praise on the part of the worshippers. It was said of Jock Troup's meetings 'he sent them home singing, because God had made them so happy.' Revivals are quite often accompanied by music and song, like the period of the Wesleys when Charles Wesley was inspired to become a prolific writer of hymns. Peter Grant wrote about the glorious prayer meetings at Grantown during revival periods.

Revivals illustrate the saying 'man's extremity is God's opportunity.' The Awakening in England in the eighteenth century came at a time when the country was plagued with poverty and hopelessness, and some historians, notably Trevelyan, argue that the aftermath of the eighteenth century revival under Whitefield and the Wesleys saved the country from the revolutionary bloodbath suffered in France. The revival in East Anglia and North-eastern Scotland in the early nineteen-twenties followed dramatic failures in 'the harvest of the sea' during a time of dreadful weather. The mixture of misery in which revival breaks through can include factors like the failure of the potato crop, or harsh treatment by landlords at the time of the Highland Clearances, or can be compounded by these elements. Alcoholic excess was a feature of community life when the Lewis Revival in 1949 occurred. The beginning of Queen Victoria's reign in 1837 marked the beginning of lean years in Strathspey. Poor harvests meant the poor had to go hungry, especially the crofters, labourers and skilled men, many of whom were in the membership of the church. The cholera epidemic in the Strathspey area in the early 1830s probably helped to turn the hearts of many of the people towards God. In Bible times, under the threat of a flood, 'Noah, when warned about things not seen, in holy fear built an ark to save his family.' (Hebrews

11 verse 7).

Hardship and emigration did not reduce the size of the congregations at Grantown. The meeting house was 'very full on Sabbath morning and afternoon, and especially so in the evening' according to Peter Grant's report for 1840. There were now six Sunday Schools and several preaching stations. A society for overseas missions was flourishing, and two young men were training as preachers. Two years later, Peter was reporting larger numbers, and a great spirit of love and unity. He was hoping for greater things following the start of a Sunday morning prayer meeting.

It is interesting to see how events at Grantown during Peter Grant's pastorate relate to the above comments on revival....

In 1834, the bright young Duncan Dunbar came home from America. (He was the reckless young dare-devil who did headstands on the parapet of the Spey Bridge). He had served there in pastorates in New Brunswick and then in New York, and was home for a visit. In his 'Sketch of my own Life and Times', written in 1844, Peter sets the scene: 'In the year 1834, the Lord visited us in mercy, poured down His Spirit, some were awakened, and just at this time we had a seasonable visit from Mr Dunbar of New York. He is a native of this place, who went to America, and became a very popular and useful minister there. He came from the land of revivals, remained some weeks, and by his lively preaching and warm appeals, (the Lord) awakened and revived the church.' There were numerous baptisms between 1834 and 1836, when 47 new members were added to the church, including four of Peter Grant's own family, to his great delight.

In 1836, ten were added to the church, and fourteen in 1837. Sixteen were added in 1838-39. 'In 1840, we had another visit from Mr Dunbar from America, and another time of refreshing from the presence of the Lord. In this year, twenty have been added to the church, mostly young people, and to my great joy, another three of my own children were among them. In 1841, thirteen were added.'

Peter gives a fuller account of events in the Report of the Baptist Home Missionary Society, 1836: 'Pray earnestly that what we have seen may be only drops before a great rain. February 1835: 'For many years we lived pretty comfortably as a church, and had a good congregation. As the church diminished by death and otherwise, the Lord from time to time called others from darkness to light to fill their places, so that our number rather increased. But although we had a name to live, perhaps as much so as the generality of professors, yet we evidently see now that much lukewarmness prevailed among us till about two years ago, when some of us consulted together, and gave ourselves to seek the Lord more fervently and earnestly by secret prayer, for the outpouring of the Spirit upon our families, and the revival of the Lord's people in general. It was OUR way to awaken professors of religion, and that they should awaken the careless; but the LORD'S way was, that He should awaken the careless, and they have awakened us. About a year and a half ago, the people manifested an unusual desire to hear the truth, so that we have had to enlarge our meeting-house. About this time last year, a few began to be concerned about their souls, but only a few, till the end of September when several were awakened. Since that time, we have been baptizing more or less every week, and others as constantly have been stirred up to the inquiry, 'What must I do to be saved?' The number added to the church since last year is twenty-six; and it is a cause of great joy that they were not old professors from other denominations, for, excepting two persons, they all lived careless about eternity. The strictest inquiry was made at their admission respecting their knowledge, experience and character. Most of them are between seventeen and thirty. There are twelve young men among them, four of them in one family. Some more are making application; others are only beginning to consider their ways. This little revival, if we may call it, was not produced by any extraordinary means, but by the Lord blessing His own Word, teaching sinners by His Spirit to sit down and count the cost, and to attend to the one thing needful.'

'We hope the awakening will become more general through the country, for as yet it has chiefly been among ourselves. But is our heart's desire and prayer to God, that our brethren of other denominations may also experience times of refreshing from the presence of the Lord. Our meeting-house is far too small. Our weekly meetings for prayer and exhortation, which used to be attended by about forty persons, have increased to one hundred and twenty. We have also opened new Sabbath Schools through the country.

April – 'I have to say that the Lord's work in this place continues to make a slow but steady progress. There is no general awakening, no crying out, no enthusiasm; everyone seems to sit down and count the cost; may they finish well! – the church is evidently making progress in life and godliness. Several are indeed fellow-helpers of the truth. One of them, who has for years been in a lifeless state, was awakened of late; he spends much of his time going from house to house, warning the wicked, directing the anxious inquirer, and comforting those that mourn, - we have fourteen young men who attend a prayer meeting every Sabbath morning. It would make you weep for joy to see them going to the house of God in company. They appear to be a band of men whom God has touched; they were all in the ranks of the enemy a few months ago. If they be strong in the grace of God, and His Word abide in them, they will help to overcome the wicked one. We have seven Sabbath Schools through the country. – Pray that the hand of the Lord may be with us, and that we may be kept blameless. A spot on any of our members at this time, like an eclipse of the sun, would draw every eye to it, and would go far to ruin us. '

During the progress of this work, Mr Grant was seized with a violent illness, during which his life was despaired of. On his recovery he writes:

'If you were afraid that the work of the Lord would be hindered by my late illness, I can say with the apostle: 'that the things which happened unto me have fallen out rather for the furtherance of the gospel.' To many the dispensation seemed to be very dark; but I was wholly resigned, and confident that in the end it would work out for good, and so it has turned out. It has awakened the church and many others to fasting and prayer. Some of the most careless lamented the opportunities which they had lost. Things are more and more promising; many are under great concern, and the awakening has become more general through the country. Two were baptized by Mr Henderson when I was hovering on the banks of Jordan. Through the tender mercies of the Lord I was enabled to resume my labours, by preaching three times yesterday, and was not the worse for it. How should I walk softly all my days, and earnestly inquire what the Lord - who raised me from the bed of death, and turned me back into the wilderness, after being to all appearance so near the land of everlasting rest – would have me to do? I was for two weeks despaired of by all; my disease was a bilious colic, which ended in inflammation of the bowels. Vain was the help of man; but the church, with brother Hutcheson, held prayer meetings continually. They then appointed a day for fasting and prayer; and before they called, the Lord answered: early that morning I fell asleep, and when I awoke found great relief, and from that time got better.'

In March 1836, he wrote to the friends and supporters of the Baptist Home Missionary Society: 'It is our humble desire and prayer for you all, that Christ may be precious to your souls, that you may sell all for the pearl of great price, and be found in Him, clothed in the white robe of His spotless righteousness in the day when He maketh up His jewels. Happy day! Happy people! Happy eternity!

'That this was a desert and solitary place, in regard to spiritual things, cannot be denied by any; that Mr Mackintosh was the first instrument in the hand of the Lord, none but a bigot will dispute; that the church since its formation enjoyed a measure of prosperity, it would be ungrateful not to acknowledge; but about two years ago, it was observed that some of the friends possessed the spirit of grace and supplication in an unusual degree. ....About eighteen months ago, the Lord began manifestly to make bare His arm in turning sinners from darkness to light, and from the power of Satan unto God. Since that time fifty-two have been added to the church ...There are several others of whom we hope well, although we have not thought it our duty yet to baptize them. A very few were lukewarm professors of religion, but most of them were living without God in the world. We have seen a most evident change on some who were formerly moral. May we not hope there was much joy in heaven over them? Does this not say to the Society, and to us their agents, Be not weary in well doing, for in due time ye shall reap, if ye faint not.'

Rev George B Duncan, a prince among preachers, gave a profile of any work of God, which has to be mentioned in relation to revival. The criteria which indicate a true work of God are seen in Acts chapter 16. The first is Obedience to God's Call (verses 6-10). The second is the Operation of God's Spirit (verses 14,18,,26,29-31) and the third is the Opposition to God's Church (verses 19-24). Peter Grant discovered this third factor in a church which had been exhibiting great love and unity in the Spirit. He wrote: 'In 1842 only three were added to the church, and in 1843 only two added... In 1842 we got the sorest trial we ever met with, (from) which we have hardly recovered yet, which was a great stumbling block in the country, and hindered the cause.' A boy made up a rhyme, drawing on the farming practice of marking sheep, about the church division that took place:

'O that the mischief-making crew
Were all reduced to one or two,
And those were painted red or blue
That everyone might know them.'

Peter continued: 'The case was this: a young man who was a member, began to make up with a girl who had no religion, and did not pretend to have any, and engaged to marry her before the church knew anything about it. When he was spoken to, he seemed to hesitate what to do. His own friends and others maintained as he promised to do what was sinful, that it was his duty to draw back and acknowledge his faults. Two of the members maintained as he had made the promise that it was his duty to perform it. It was evident that his mind was all along going that way, so he married, and was excommunicated. All his father's family were in the church, and they and a few others insisted that the two men who thought he should perform his promise should be excommunicated, or at least be made to make a public confession before the church. To this the church would not yield. We wrote to other churches about it, and almost all of them were of the opinion like the two men that he should fulfil his promise. His friends became dissatisfied, maintained that there was no discipline in the church, began to find fault with our doctrine; nothing pleased them, so they left us. His father, two brothers, and six women set up a separate meeting, regardless of the consequences. Lord, what is man, if left to himself a single day? This was the first division we ever had in the church, and although those who separated were few in number, as their leader was a young man of piety and talents, they continued for a number of years, though without anyone joining them, till they dwindled away to nothing. But their division was a great stumbling block to the people around us, so that for the next six years, we only baptized on average three every year, but one good has come out of the evil. No one afterward attempted to make a division, as everyone saw how low they brought themselves, and that their leader spoiled his talents and hindered his usefulness.'

Fresh developments came in 1848. Peter Grant's third son, William, came to join his father in the work at Grantown, supported by the Baptist Home Missionary Society, after three years study with Rev Shearer in Fortrose, and two years' study in Dr Chalmer's classes in Edinburgh. Peter was delighted to have William alongside him. Peter wrote: 'Soon afterward the Lord of His free unmerited favour began to revive His work among us again by the outpouring of His Spirit. He made the word effectual to the salvation of many souls, and we enjoyed a glorious time of refreshing from the presence of the Lord.'

On 20 August, they baptized four young girls in the River Spey, including Peter's youngest daughter Christina. The congregation on the river bank numbered about 500. A month later eight were baptized before a congregation of about 1000 people. October saw twenty more baptized, and Peter gave up trying to estimate the number present. In November they baptized fourteen, and in December, five. In January 1859, seven were baptized and three in March, and twelve in April. Peter Grant wrote: 'Through the whole of 1849 and the beginning of 1850, about one hundred have been added to the church, men and women of all ages, some very young, some very old, some hard-hearted sinners were converted, but a great deal of them were persons of the best moral character, who were led to see that morality or formality would avail nothing, without being new creatures in Christ, and a few who were believers before, had seen it their duty to be baptized according to the primitive order that Christ left in His church, and to the glory of that grace which did so great things for us, we have to state that at the end of three or four years that with few exceptions, they have continued to adorn the doctrine of God our Saviour.'
Even in the depths of winter this spate of river baptisms continued.

The physical demands on minister and candidates must have been considerable, for in those days each baptism was a triple affair, with separate immersions in the name of each Person of the Trinity.

Reports in the Baptist Magazine in 1848 and 1849 reveal Peter's reactions to these events, which he viewed as an on-going process of divine origin. He wrote:

'....Numbers are under deep impression. Many continue to make application, who profess to have 'passed from death unto life'. But we endeavour to be more careful than ever we have been what characters we receive. Sometimes all the members of the church are engaged at once speaking to enquirers. We have enquirers at our house every evening. Our weekly meetings, which used to be held in a private room, now fill our meeting-house twice on week evenings.

'On Sabbath, multitudes must stand outside, or go home for want of room. There is certainly excitement, but no crying, nor enthusiasm of any kind – nothing but sober-minded people seeing it wise and reasonable to attend to the concerns of their immortal souls.....It is like a stream that has been accumulating for years, which has at last broken through the banks, and has come upon us like a flood.'

As Peter put it later 'Revivals have been of great benefit to the churches of Christ, where conducted in a Scriptural way, depending on the grace of God.'

In a letter to William, on August 7, 1844, Peter reveals something of the theology of salvation which underpins his preaching, in a draft of a letter to an opponent which he shares with his son:

'Dear Brother, You impose a heavy task on me, when you desire me to try to convince you, that your views are erroneous about the atonement.
All I can pretend in that respect is to pray that the Lord will lead you and myself also to receive with meekness the engrafted Word which is able to save our souls – as to your view of the atonement, I would say little about that, only that you do not consider the length to which it would lead you, to be consistent, but if it leads you to deny God's sovereignty, His electing love, that he works to will and to do of His good pleasure, that salvation is of the Lord from first to last, I am sorry for it. I know it is a duty to preach the Gospel to every creature, and when I address men I am fully warranted to warn, call, invite and beseech all to be reconciled to God, that there is a fullness in Christ, all things ready, enough to spare – but can I overlook all the Scriptures that speak of God as having chosen His people in Christ, Ephesians 1v3, Romans 9, providing a kingdom for them before the foundation of the world Matth 25, saved, bought, washed them with His blood, all things are of God 2 Cor 5, to will and to do.

Phil 2. He gives faith Jude 3, and draws to Christ John 6. convinces, enlightens, converts by His Spirit etc. You then call upon me to reconcile this doctrine with man's responsibility – I readily confess this is beyond my present ability, although I know they are reconcilable. Men of the greatest minds of every age have attempted it, but in general they were obliged to exclaim with Paul, O the depth of it. – so the most candid have satisfied themselves with speaking as the Scripture speaks on both sides. May I not ask you how you will reconcile your own views with the doctrines contained in the passages on the other side.

Dr Wardlaw wrote a book upon (it), proving that man has the ability if he had the will, but will man change his will, or will the natural man receive the things of the Spirit – has Christ bought with His own blood a people He will not save, or if you hold to the new doctrine that He did not make atonement for any man, but only to satisfy justice – it will not deliver you out of one difficulty if the Spirit and grace of God is necessary for the application of the atonement, and if that grace is given to some and not to others, you have election still. As for such Scriptures as Christ being for the propitiation for the sins of the whole world, a ransom for all, etc. we understand it to mean Jews and Gentiles, (to) take it otherwise it proves too much, how many passages of Scripture speak of Christ as coming to save the world – to draw all men to Him - and no one among us will suppose that the whole will be saved, which I was stirred up by some of your own remarks, and even made mention of them.' or that all will be drawn to Christ.

'Dear brother, I only write these few things wishing you to be cautious in adopting or stating your views of any new theory, however plausible at first sight. Philosophers and even we ourselves see things in the kingdom of nature and we cannot fathom their depth, and shall we wonder, then, that sometimes to us clouds and darkness may surround the throne of God, while at the same time justice goeth before His face.'

'Dear William, you will judge for yourself whether it is best to transcribe these things, or alter them as you like and send them to Thomson, or whether it is best to let him alone at present…

May the Lord hold up your goings and lead you in the right way that you may come at last to a city of habitation is the prayer of your affectionate Father, Peter Grant.'

I have included this lengthy passage from one letter for several reasons. It reveals the kind of Biblical presuppositions behind Peter's preaching of the Gospel. It demonstrates his gracious approach to someone whose views differ from him.

It shows his humility in submitting what he writes to editorial amendment by William. It reveals the intimacy of the relationship between Peter Grant and his third son, the preacher.

Finally, in the light of his busy schedule, how did he get time to think and write in such depth and detail?!

In 1851, by the favour of Lord Seafield, and his new factor, land was obtained for the erection of the first purpose-built church. The new building stood in the High Street, and could seat nearly 400 people. It cost £298, all of which was raised before the opening day. £100 was raised in Grantown, and the rest came in response to a preaching tour undertaken by William when he visited Edinburgh, Glasgow, Aberdeen and Elgin, as well as other intermediate places. The preacher at the opening on 19 September 1851 was Dr James Paterson from Glasgow, one of the foremost Scottish Baptists of the day. The number of church members in communion rose to one hundred and eighty-four.

It is right to mention the development of the work and ministry at Grantown in relation to wider issues. The great 1859 Revival found Peter Grant alert and ready. He had been reading with great interest news of the revival in Ulster and the United States. Its effects were not felt in the North-East of Scotland until the very end of the year, but in the spring of 1860, eight members of the Grantown church united with a small group from Elgin to form Forres Baptist Church. This church continued for about fifty years, giving a strong evangelical witness for most of that time. One of its later ministers, AC Sievewright, was instrumental in the formation of Inverness Baptist Church.

The church organisations grew naturally, under the good direction of Peter Grant. In 1831 he started a Sunday School. It was a great success, and was attended by almost all the young people of the town. Branch Sunday Schools opened in the surrounding area. There were five by 1853, seven by 1854 and eight in 1857. There was also a large Total Abstinence Society, formed in 1854. Peter's son, William, conducted a young people's Bible Class with a regular weekly attendance of seventy.

Peter worked with Willam Hutcheson of Kingussie to maintain a vigorous itinerant ministry. In the early summer of 1842, they undertook a preaching tour to Badenoch, Inverness, Kiltarlity, Fortrose and Beauly. Peter became ill, and had to return home in June. When he recovered, he was back at work on the harvest at Ballentua, but as soon as this was complete, he was off on a three-week preaching tour of Buchan. The following year, aged 60, he was no less energetic, both in Grantown, and throughout the whole North-East of Scotland.

We shall say more about the Clearances later, but there was a small but steady flow of losses through emigration, mainly to Canada, although others went to the United States, South Africa, Australia and New Zealand. After Peter Grant's death, the 1870s saw the opening up of the prairies to farming in America, and the losses to the Grantown membership became difficult to replace.

CHAPTER TEN –
REVIVAL REPORTED
BAPTIST HOME MISSIONARY SOCIETY

In this chapter, we will confine ourselves to Peter's descriptions of events in reports and correspondence, and in letters to his daughter Christina and William.

Report for Baptist Home Missionary Society, June 1839: 'Our country, along with the rest of the Highlands, has been afflicted during the last three years for want of bread. The poor, the labourer, and tradesman are suffering, and of these our church is composed; but they rejoice in the God of their salvation….As a church, we are as comfortable as we have ever been, but we need the outpouring of the Holy Spirit to give us more life, activity and zeal. I have always approved of using means to promote revivals, if conducted in a Scriptural way.'

March 1840. 'There are about sixteen Sabbath Schools in different parts of the area, averaging about thirty scholars, some old, some young. Six of these schools belong to our church, and the rest belong to the Establishment….Another symptom of life among us is, that in the midst of our poverty we have commenced a Missionary Society.

October 1840: 'Since I last wrote, the Lord in mercy visited us with a time of refreshing from His presence. It came upon us unexpectedly. We had used no extraordinary efforts of any kind, were just entering the bustle of harvest, and had little prospect of seeing much of the goodness of the Lord, at least before winter. But the Lord's ways are not our ways; in the most busy season, our meeting-house began to be crowded in an unusual manner, both on Sabbath and week-days. The church was revived; hardened and careless sinners were alarmed, and it became evident that the Spirit of the Lord was amongst us. This commenced with a visit from Mr Dunbar of New York, a native of this place. When he saw the grace of God he was glad, and preached among us for three weeks; he then left us; but the Lord did not leave us. Multitudes come to hear the truth. And every week some take warning to flee from the wrath to come, and find refuge in the blood of Christ.

Since the beginning of July, fourteen have been baptized, and many are soon expected to follow. But the best of my story (at least to myself) is still to be told. Three of my own children were among the baptized, and I am now the happy father who has seen seven of my children putting on the Lord Jesus Christ. O! that I could praise the Lord for His goodness, and live and die unto the Lord.'

December 1840: 'The church is revived – prayer meetings are multiplied - more Sabbath Schools are commenced – our meeting-house, which seats about three hundred, is crowded. Our new members give us great pleasure; eighteen of them were, till lately, living without God in the world.'
March 1841: 'Our present number is 160, and although they are poor in this world, I hope they are rich in faith, and their simplicity, union and love is a great comfort to me. Where much of the Spirit of Christ is possessed, little ruling is necessary; when the love of Christ prevails in a church, it crucifies the flesh with its affections and lusts'....
'May the Lord abundantly pour out His Spirit of grace and supplication upon our benevolent friends, and upon us who occupy their talents as well as our own! We might then expect to see great things. If we compare the Highlands of Scotland with what they were forty years ago, we exclaim, 'What hath God wrought! Let us serve our generation by the will of God, that those who come after us may enter into our labours with the fields white unto harvest.'

March 1842: 'We have still to acknowledge the goodness of the Lord, that He has not forsaken us; to him be all the glory. We have also had our trials, But our meeting-house was never better filled.... When there is moonlight, and the people are not too busy, I generally preach twice on week-days, and attend two prayer meetings. I have twelve (preaching) stations, one of them 24 miles away....I have often been afraid that many of our churches do not hold up the hands of their pastors as they should do; not that I have any reason to complain, but from what I hear of other places. The Lord grant that we may be of the meek of the earth, that the Lord may guide us in judgement, and teach us His way.'

January 1843: 'I think I have laboured more this winter than for some time past. My health was good, and there is a good deal of life among the brethren. For six weeks back, I had a sermon, or held a prayer meeting

almost every evening of the week, excepting Saturday. When the harvest was over, I went to Buchan, and preached in many places during the three weeks I remained. The congregations were generally crowded.'
December 1843: 'Last Sabbath, we baptized a young man in the River Spey, and although there was a heavy storm on the ground, hundreds of people assembled, and behaved with great solemnity.'

Extract from letter from Peter to William, 21 December 1843: 'The only noise in this country is the Free Church. Mr McLeod preaches every Sabbath in the wood west from Grantown to upwards of 2000 people. He preaches once a week day in our meeting-house. They are petitioning for wood to build, and a stance to build upon. It is thought that they will get a place at Bridge of Dalnain. The Free Church has not thinned our congregation in the least as yet. They hold a meeting in a private room on Sabbath evening; our meeting is crowded, but with all this stir I don't see or hear of any concerned about their souls…

The Committee reported in 1844:
'During the past year, twenty-eight preachers have been employed by the Society, many Sabbath Schools have been conducted, and numbers of tracts distributed.

'The fields are white unto harvest…. Let all the friends of Jesus remember that the time is short – the night is far spent – the day is at hand; all require to be excited to exertion. Believers, indeed, have now the anticipation of that rest which remains for the people of God, but they are taught not to sleep as do others, but diligently to occupy the talents entrusted to them until the Lord comes.'

Letter to William, from Congash near Grantown, 31 December 1844:
'My Dear William, A Happy New Year to you, and much of the grace that makes all things new. I received your letter last week, which made my heart right glad, to find that above all study you are studying the Word of God, and that you are not withering like a transplanted tree, which many students do for a while at best, when they begin the study of languages…I am truly glad…that you have a goodly heritage among the few but pious people of Fortrose. (William was studying with Mr Shearer at Fortrose).

Letter to William, Wednesday January 31, 1844: ' as a church we are very comfortable, a number of the members are more lively than when you left us, and the few distant and cold are coming nearer. I will not venture to say much, but I am just of the opinion that we are at the eve of a revival less or more, which would be a great mercy if the Lord would grant it. I gave a private serious address to the church last Sabbath.

Baptist Home Missionary Society Report, June 1845: As a church, we go on very comfortably, in love and union…There is a great struggle going on between the two Churches of Scotland, as they call themselves. Our greatest difficulty is to draw the minds of the people from this fearful struggle, to the concerns of their precious souls….

'During summer I visited Fortrose, Elgin, Huntly, Aberdeen, St Fergus, New Pitsligo, and several places in Morayshire and Banffshire. Upon the whole, the truth is gaining ground. I believe there never was in our day greater need of men who can and will declare the whole counsel of God.'

Baptist Home Missionary Report, 1848: 'real conversions are few and far between; yet, after looking seven times, we see a little cloud like a man's hand, which encourages us to hope that showers of blessing – which will cause the desert to blossom as the rose – are not far off.
March – Christians appear at present to be hanging their harps on the willows; but God will arise, and have mercy on Zion. We have seen marvellous things, and we know the end of these wonders will be to bring about glorious and happy days.

'I always preach three sermons on Sabbath, and attend the school, which numbers 100 children, and would greatly increase, if we could get teachers; but our men have often schools through the country, which they must attend. We have a number of stations within 12 or 15 miles of Grantown, which I endeavour to supply on week evenings, especially in winter, besides attending two weekly prayer meetings; but without help, I could not leave Grantown for one Sabbath, in present circumstances.
'As my son was home in summer, I took some extensive journeys, but the chief part of our labour was in the surrounding country, in which we preached to immense congregations.' (He was then 65 years old – GJM).

The 1849 Report contained a thrilling and detailed account from Peter Grant of the Lord at work in the Grantown area:

'The Lord has been graciously pleased to pour out His Spirit on this station. …we have often been cast down ourselves, labouring so long, and seeing comparatively little fruit; but we encouraged ourselves with the thought, that there is joy in heaven over ONE sinner that repenteth.

'When we entered the field, we doubted not that we should require for a long time to be casting our bread upon the waters. About fifty years ago, the Highlands of Scotland, except a few favoured spots, where a pious minister happened to be placed, were as ignorant of true religion as heathens, or as England was when the Bible was chained to the pulpit…

'By the blessing of God upon our own and other societies, these evils have, in great measure, been removed, and the fields seem white unto harvest.

What has been done already is far from lost labour; hundreds have given clear evidence of having passed from death unto life; many have died in hope of a glorious resurrection; poverty has forced others to emigrate to foreign lands, where we hope they are still shining as lights in the world; and a number of churches will remain endeavouring to hold forth the truth, and the ordinances of the house of God, as they were delivered by Christ and His apostles.

'What has taken place here for some months back , encourages us to hope that the Lord is about to arise and have mercy on Zion, and that the desert will blossom and bud like the rose….In August last, the Lord in mercy turned our captivity like streams in the south, and the little cloud, that first appeared like a man's hand, poured such blessings on precious souls, as convinced all that it was the doing of the Lord. It was marvellous in our eyes, and will be long remembered in this place…..We saw more than ever the wisdom of the great Redeemer, in sending out His disciples two and two to preach the Gospel, when the Society allowed my son to labour with me in this place. We have had an opportunity of supplying our preaching stations far and near; and at times, to supply other churches, and this at a time when the people could best attend, while the church and people in Grantown have not been neglected for a single day....

About this time it was beginning to appear that the prayers of the brethren were more earnest and full of unction. Some individuals appeared to be more lively; one woman particularly manifested more spirituality and activity; and it is very remarkable that two of her daughters were the first brought to concern about their souls. About this time, a discourse was preached from 'Awake, awake, put on strength, O arm of the Lord', and soon after, four young girls, who had long struggled with convictions, at length revealed their minds, and, after much tribulation, found joy and peace in believing. As two of them resided on the banks of the River Spey, in a most convenient place, we thought it proper to have a public baptism. Having given intimation of this, we expected a good number to attend, although it was early on a Sabbath morning, but, to our astonishment, more than a thousand people gathered around us, to whom we preached repentance toward God, and faith in our Lord Jesus Christ, with the duty of believers to be immersed in the name of the Holy Trinity. By the solemnity with which they witnessed what took place, by the impressions visibly made, and the manner in which our meeting-house was filled afterwards, we were convinced that the Spirit of the Lord was at work. After that day, souls were awakened at almost every sermon and prayer-meeting, inquirers became numerous, the church was revived, and many began in earnest to look to the Shepherd and Bishop of their souls.

'Seeing the good effect of the above public baptism, we appointed another, 20 September, at which time my son delivered an affecting address to at least twelve hundred people....

'The revival continued with increasing interest; and we continued our public baptisms as long as the weather permitted the people to assemble in the open air. For no house was near to contain the multitudes that came from all parts of the country....

'We hope that no-one will suppose that we attach undue importance to baptism, or give it a place that the Scriptures do not; no, our first concern is to see souls converted, the careless awakened, the formalist convinced of his error, and the wounded led to the Lamb of God; we have every reason to conclude that such were those whom we have baptized.

We are, however, more convinced than ever of the utility of baptism in its own place. The experience of fifty years has taught us the necessity of being as careful as possible in the reception of members. Nothing can be more hurtful to the persons received, or to the church receiving, than the admission of such as are strangers to the grace of God. We have, consequently, several who are still kept back, owing to circumstances, of whom we hope well, some of them very young; we have received three of fourteen years, and one of twelve. We have five flourishing Sunday Schools through the country. The one in Grantown is very interesting; about a hundred children, under twelve years of age attend. My son, who has a particular talent for instructing the young, meets the children twice a week, an hour before our prayer-meeting, when he teaches them to sing psalms and hymns; and as all is gratis, a great many attend, and many of them wait until the meeting is over. In some cases, they bring their parents along with them, Some of whom, we trust, have reaped benefits to their souls. 'Under the mighty hand of God, it is our prayer-meetings that hold our souls in life. More than a hundred people, besides children, have attended our prayer-meetings twice a week since the revival began, and our present prospects are fully as encouraging as at any former period. The Lord accompanies His Word by the power of His Spirit, He wounds and He heals. Inquirers are many; four found peace to their minds last week.

'Monday last we had our prayer meeting, and such a prayer meeting we never saw – three hundred people, young and old, attended. Many were deeply affected. 'The doctrine preached is repentance toward God, and faith in the Lord Jesus Christ; man's depravity and helplessness; and the free and full salvation of Christ to all that believe: God's sovereignty and efficacious grace; and man's responsibility.

But we do not mention these things to seek or take any glory to ourselves; we could not, though we were inclined, the work is so manifestly of the Lord; we used no extraordinary effort, and there is no very great excitement, but the good work goes gradually and steadily forward, and the people begin to see that the concerns of the soul ought to be attended to above every other concern. Our object in writing this sketch is to encourage our dear friends who support the Society, and strengthen our brethren in other parts, who are bearing the burden and heat of the day, to labour without fainting.

'Dear Brethren, pray for us, bless the Lord, and let us exalt His name together, not only for the many souls that we have reason to hope have everlasting benefit, but that those who have made a profession are everything we could wish, and that the Lord has preserved us from any erroneous doctrine sweeping in among us, which would be very pernicious in our present state. We are all in unity and love.' March 4, 1849: I have no thought that our revival is at a stand; after our chapel was crowded, multitudes remained outside till we dismissed those within, and the house filled again; we hope the Lord was among us. I went to preach in a distant part of the country, and left William in Grantown. After sermon, I had to converse with some about their souls, so that it was about midnight before I got home; but late as it was, some who were at sermon at Grantown waited for me, and would not go to bed till I had conversed with them. With several the church are satisfied, many others are under concern. Blessed be the Lord. Pray for us.

April 15, 1849: 'O that we could render to the Lord in some measure according to His goodness…the revival is spreading to our out-stations on every hand; our Sabbath Schools are prosperous, our prayer-meetings are throng and solemn, often more than 200 persons. A kind of awe has fallen on the multitude, and those who feel no interest in the cause acknowledge that there is something in it that they do not understand. Yesterday we baptized seven in the presence of more than 1000 people. Some came from a distance of nearly twenty miles to hear and see it. From the beginning we have resolved not to go out of our usual way, to create excitement; so I hope our revival may continue the longer, and that the Lord will preserve us from falling into that deadness which often follows revivals.

'Our greatest disadvantage is want of room in our meeting-place; If things continue as they are, when the warm days come, we must meet in the open air; but I hope we shall not complain – the great end is obtained, souls are converted, we hope God is glorified. Angels rejoice. The church is alive in unity and love. I wish we had you here, we have a number of the young panting for knowledge.'

CHAPTER ELEVEN –
GAELIC – MOTHER TONGUE AND
LANGUAGE OF THE HEART

Peter Grant was a Gael, through and through. Gaelic was still spoken widely in the northern Highlands in his time, and, of course, in the Hebrides. Many of his fellow Gaels would not have been literate in English or, indeed, in Gaelic, and for this reason the spoken word, set to music, was a very important means of communication. Song could be used very effectively in the proclamation of the Gospel. Peter Grant would also have been well aware that religious bodies had been active in the Highlands and Islands, implanting the seeds of Christian knowledge more than a century before he himself began preaching, and that he could secure the message in minds that were not always entirely ignorant of some of the basic principles of the Christian faith.

Attempts were made to use schools to speed religious knowledge and instruction in Scotland, and school societies had a special interest in the Highlands and Islands. The Scottish Society for the Propagation of Christian Knowledge was founded in 1709, and the General Assembly gave moral and financial support for its work. Unfortunately, the Society forbade the use of Gaelic in its programmes until 1776. Even then, the Gaelic language was viewed as a source of superstition and savagery. The funds for promotion of Gaelic never exceeded £2000 per annum.

Despite this, the first Scottish Gaelic New Testament was produced in 1761, and the first Scottish Gaelic Bible was printed in 1801. By the 1830s, financial support reached £4000 per annum, and SSPCK had 10 missionaries, 33 catechists and 261 teachers at work.

The Paisley Society for Gaelic Missions used itinerant missionaries, and the Gaelic Schools Societies founded schools in Edinburgh, Glasgow, Dundee and Inverness in the 1810s and 1820s. They taught Gaelic literacy as a means of accessing the Word of God in the mother tongue.

It was hard for Highland Gaels to break free from traditional loyalties. They kept hoping that their landlords would act justly if only they were fully aware of circumstances. The Gaelic poetry of the nineteenth century tends to blame factors and farmers rather than individual landowners for their woeful circumstances. When the Gaels had to migrate to the cities, Gaelic speaking often died out within a generation.

It is against this background that we have to view the life of Peter Grant. Peter's language context was entirely Gaelic until he was twelve. He developed good English skills, but he drilled his family in Gaelic, and his third son, William, was fluent in Gaelic and succeeded him in the pastorate at Grantown on Spey Baptist Church.

Song and verse were deeply engrained in the Gaels. Gaelic poetic forms are ancient and complex, and traditionally the Gaelic bards were well-trained, imaginative and intelligent. The sound structures of the language mean that rhyme was important, as were repetition, alliteration and rhythm. With the older, more learned tradition of verse, which was cultivated until the sixteenth century, quatrains of a set number of syllables per line were employed by the poets, with numerous different metrical forms, often decked out with internal rhyming schemes which use cross-rhymes in the couplets, and the first syllable or word or phrase of the poem is generally repeated to signal its conclusion. Praise poetry was a sub-section of the secular Gaelic literature, and the title 'file', plural 'filid', meaning originally 'learned poet', is derived from a root meaning 'to see'.

Peter Grant's hymns, however, operated within the tradition of Gaelic popular song or 'òran'. He himself was known as 'Pàruig Grannd nan Oran' ('Peter Grant of the Songs'), his 'songs' being of a spiritual, rather than a secular, kind. They were 'hymns' of a particular sort.

The Strathspey News of September 4, 1926 carried a report of a memorial service for Rev Peter Grant. One of the speakers (possibly Rev J Grant Robinson) at the service said: 'We (the Gaels) possess a rich inheritance of national music, and national song, and a national history starry with saints and heroes and famous deeds. And not least, the race has been endowed with great poets, and of these among the latest, some of the greatest. The famous hills of Glenorchy gave to our Highland tongue Duncan Ban Macintyre, the supreme Poet of Scenery. Rannoch, and the gloomy glens of

Perthshire gave us the magnificent genius of Dugald Buchanan. Then later still these braes of Strathspey produced this sweet lyric poet, Peter Grant with his happy strains and his new idealism.'

The Scottish Baptist Magazine describes Peter Grant as 'a sort of combined Moody and Sankey; he composed and sang his own hymns, and he delivered the message of the Gospel with much power.'

Revival movements have often expressed their spiritual emotions in hymns, in the Wesleyan or Welsh Revivals for instance, and here in the Peter Grant era, by Highland firesides. His songs bridged the Baptist and Presbyterian communities in Strathspey and the wider Highlands and Islands, and eventually took on Transatlantic and Australian dimensions.

Peter Grant's contribution to Gaelic poetry expressed in hymns is small in volume, but very significant and influential in content. In his 'Brief Sketch' of his father's life, his son William tells how, soon after his conversion to Christ, Peter Grant was filled with compassion for his perishing friends and fellow-countrymen. William writes:

'Dressed in kilt and tartan bonnet, he went forth almost every evening to some cottage to tell of Jesus' love; so that in a few years he became an acceptable preacher, and for sixty years he was very successful in attracting and arresting large audiences. He felt deeply grieved to find that his countrymen at wakes and weddings, were in the habit of spending whole nights in singing silly and even immoral songs, so he applied himself to the composition of spiritual songs, sung (in Gaelic) to the airs familiar to the people.

He often sang a new poem after a week night service, which attracted crowds, gave him the ear of the people, and made him popular in the homes of the poor. Peter Grant's spiritual songs proved so popular that the first edition of them was published when he was 26 years old, in 1809.'

The collection eventually consisted of thirty-nine poems, and passed through twenty editions and many reprints. His son William wrote: 'He had the satisfaction of seeing them supplant the ballads of the people. They have been used as the means of conversion of hundreds, besides being the source of refreshing and edification of thousands of God's children.' The tenth edition of the songs was published in 1863, by Mr Collie of Edinburgh, and they were 'eagerly sought after in Australia and Canada, and wherever the roaming Highlander has penetrated. Their charm seems to lie in some measure of genuine poetry, combined with a rich vein of Gospel marrow, expressed in the terse and pathetic ('emotional' GJM) language of the common people.' Part of this dimension of influence has been Christian discussion in prose and poetry of our relationship and reaction to God and the world.

The 'Dàin Spioradail' went through twenty editions, dating from 1809 until 1903, expanding to thirty-nine songs. The date of the original edition was made known by the author in his preface to the fifth edition published in 1837, where he states that the first edition was published 28 years earlier, i.e. in 1809. The various editions were printed in Inverness, Edinburgh, Elgin, and Fayetteville (North Carolina) in 1826, and in Montreal in 1836. The British Museum has three editions, and Glasgow University Library has two, with the eighth (1857) edition corrected throughout and some notes added.

In his study "The Glory of the Lamb': The Gaelic Hymns of Peter Grant", Professor Donald Meek shows how Biblical faith and local culture became married and contextualised in Grant's Gaelic hymns. One of the most popular of his songs was 'Gloir an Uain' ('The Glory of the Lamb'), sung to a well-known secular tune. Here are three verses translated by Donald Meek:

'Zion is singing as sweetly as possible,
Giving a thousand honours to the Lamb,
Singing of His love that will never change
- it saved her wholly from perdition.
An eternal hallelujah sounds from heaven's host
That surrounds the throne of the King,
And that too is the sound that will melt the hearts
Of those on earth who follow the Lamb.

The Son of God deserves obedience and honour
Since He Himself suffered death;
It was He who perceived our need and predicament ,
And it was He who pitied our plight;

He Himself bore all the lashings
Through which we now have been saved,
And His wounds and sores cry out together
That each creature should give Him respect.

Your love from the start was wondrously free
To poor people who were totally lost,
When You came down with Gospel's sound
And no-one deserved your love;
We were without God, without shelter or home,
With no order, or refuge from wrath,
While His curse was eternally driving us homewards
To an ocean of burning flames.

One of the tenderest of his poems throbs with human sensitivity, and yet it put Peter in the firing line with 'The Men', a group of arbiters of theological correctness within the Highland ranks of the Church of Scotland. The poem is called 'The Young Child in Heaven', and it tells the story of a mother wakening to discover that her child is dying. This was a real experience in Highland communities, and the poem touched many hearts. Lachlan Macbean, editor of the 'Fifeshire Advertiser' translated several of Peter Grants songs. Here is Lachlan Macbean's translation of two of its verses:

'She woke with a start,
Crying 'Love of my heart!
'What ails thee? Thou art not dead!'
And she fondled me so,
She would not let me go,
Till my life, ebbing low, had fled.

'When they closed my young eyes,
Angels came from the skies,
And they made me to rise above.
Oh! swift was our flight,
Through the valleys of night,
And I now dwell in light and love.'

Peter Grant had a firm and certain belief in the child's salvation, possibly based on texts like Genesis 18 verse 25; 'Will not the Judge of all the earth do right?' Peter's allusion in the poem to the child's acceptance by God as in a state of blameless innocence was viewed by 'The Men' as tainted with error. They would have argued from Psalm 51 verse 4: 'Surely I was sinful at birth, sinful from the time my mother conceived me.' Peter Grant's view would, I guess, have been grounded in the mercy of God, and the merits of the Cross of Christ, being exercised proleptically in the case of infants.

Grant's song shows his willingness to tackle thorny subjects, especially in a society with frighteningly bad infant mortality rates. Donald Meek writes that 'nevertheless, its hauntingly beautiful tune and consoling message have given it an enduring place beyond the churches. The BBC holds a fine recording of the song being sung by one of Gaeldom's best-known secular singers, Calum Kennedy, and it is often heard on radio programmes.'

Peter Grant's 'Song on the Missionaries' expresses our responsibility to take the Gospel overseas. He was well aware that the Baptist Home Missionary Society for Scotland, to which he belonged, was part of a wider global effort to present the Christian message beyond British shores, represented most obviously (for Baptists) in William Carey's missionary activity in Bengal. Here is Donald Meek's translation:

'Is it not a cause of sadness for you to consider the hosts who are dead, and who put their hope in dumb idols; but who will to give them a message about the Lamb, over sea and oceans, and a rugged road?

'Listen to the young people who have become so brave, that they say with joy, 'We are the ones who will go, if you consider we have received grace, and gift, and talent that will be of benefit to them.

'But we will go northwards to the frozen oceans, and to the mountains covered in great snow. Among the mountains we will find a multitude, where no summer has come which has melted their cloak.

'They have a cold heart with no pity for anything, (facing) destruction and perdition, every hour without peace; it is their custom, as was once that of Highlanders, that the one is the strongest who subdues the rest.'

'But when they receive knowledge of the glory of the Lamb, they will have ample love for Him and for His people; their holiness will grow, and they will have beauty and warmth that would put to shame those who make cold professions.'

In his Preface to the Fourth Edition of Dan Spioradail, Peter Grant reveals his inner motivation for writing the Songs:

'Singing is practised by almost every nation under heaven, and it has been found in every age to have a powerful operation upon the mind – to elevate it above trivial things - to comfort it under afflictions and trials – to banish sorrows and cares – and to strengthen the heart for great achievements. Christians are not only invited to this cheerful exercise, but positively commanded, to teach and admonish one another with psalms and hymns, and spiritual songs, singing and making melody to the Lord, with grace in their hearts – Colossians 3 verse 10. And we have seen with our eyes that where true religion in a prosperous state, there is singing and the voice of gladness in the dwellings of the righteous – Psalm 118 verse 15; and seldom can a company (particularly young pious people) meet without joining their voices together, to sing the praises of God. On the other hand, when the children of Zion hang their harps on the willow trees, and cannot sing the songs of Zion, it is one proof that they are too near Babel streams, and not drinking abundantly out of the river that makes glad the city of our God.

'When the morning stars sang together, all the sons of God shouted for joy – Job 38 verse 7; and shouting for joy will be part of the joyful work of the saints in the eternal world.

'The Highlands of Scotland have been notable for singing in ages past, and a number of men appeared among them who had the best of talents for poetry; but alas, true piety, self-denial, and devotedness to God, were little known among them; and then, their beautiful talents for poetry were prostituted for the worst of purposes – for the praise of some men and the disgrace of others; and their vain and profane songs were awfully corrupting the morals of the youth, who took the greatest delight in them. And their brethren in other places who enjoyed the Gospel in its purity for ages, neglected the Highlanders, although they were a very interesting race of men, and always found among the bravest and best defenders of our country.

'At last, like Moses, it came into the hearts of some to visit their brethren – societies were established – the Scriptures were circulated – preachers were sent forth – and Gaelic schools were instituted – and now, by the blessing of the Lord it is well known that their labour was not in vain. It was a glorious day for the Highlanders when the Scriptures, the psalms and hymns, were translated into their native tongue; but hitherto they had no spiritual songs that they could sing in private, and with their old Highland airs, till Dugald Buchanan of Rannoch appeared, a father in Israel. He spent his time and his talents in teaching them to read, preaching the Gospel to them, and composing spiritual songs for their edification and comfort. His poems have not yet been equalled and will never be excelled. Many thousand copies of his little book have been sold, but his race was run before he composed such a variety as would suit Christians in every situation.

'About twelve years ago I composed a few poems, and by the advice of some friends, published them. As to their merit, it is not for me to judge, only they got a wide circulation; and good judges say, that if they do no good, they will do no harm; and it is well known that in every part of the Highlands they are sung, and a vain song is seldom heard....

'Some have been saying that I published them for my temporal benefit, but I hope I have a higher aim; and those with whom I was dealing know that it was very little profit that I ever reaped from the sale of them. That souls may reap the benefit, and the Lord may have the glory, is the desire and prayer of your servant, Peter Grant.'

In his preface to the sixth edition in 1842, Peter Grant wrote that 'it was to be published in a cheap form, so that most of the poor Highlanders may buy copies for themselves, and that those who cannot, may be supplied gratis by their rich neighbours, who wish to see the poor rich in faith.' Peter's great-grandson, Rev J Grant-Robinson, Perth Baptist Church, said many years later: 'He did not cultivate his poetic genius for the sake of poetry, nor did he sing hymns for the sake of putting beautiful sentiments into beautiful language. He sang that others might sing – his own heart was full of gladness and of the peace of God.'

Someone, possibly Mr N McNeil, wrote the following appeal for funding to allow Peter Grant to employ help on the farm. The memoir gives a clear insight into his Gaelic and Highland context, his reputation as a Christian preacher and a Gaelic poet, and his standing in the Strathspey community:

'MEMOIR of Mr PETER GRANT, at Grantown, in Strathspey.

Mr Peter Grant, a farmer in the Highlands, is a member of the church under the pastoral care of Mr Lachlan McIntosh, at Grantown. He possesses peculiar gifts for usefulness, not only to his brethren, but to his countrymen in the Highlands; and Christians of various denominations agree in bearing their testimony in his favour, as a zealous and faithful servant of Jesus Christ. For a considerable time past, Mr Grant has been employed, as actively as occasion would permit, in publishing to his countrymen the 'glad tidings of great joy.' He also possesses a poetical genius, and his muse, following the bent of his mind, has employed herself in arranging, in the dress of numbers, some of the Gospel history and doctrines. These simple sonnets have been very generally circulated through the Highlands, and have greatly supplanted the profane songs and ballads formerly very common there; so that a traveller, if he be alive to divine things, will be delighted with hearing some of the great truths of the Gospel sung by many a country girl in strains so simple and artless cannot fail to excite a peculiar interest, and which, it is hoped, may, in not a few instances, be owned of God as the instruments of leading those who hear them, to a saving knowledge of the truth as it is in Jesus. Thus the love of music which characterises the Highlanders is judiciously made subservient to the advancement of their eternal interests; and long after he is numbered with the dead, the knowledge of the Gospel may be kept alive by means of these humble songs, and the blessings of salvation may descend to succeeding ages.

Mr Grant supports himself and his family by cultivating a small farm, which, with much laborious industry, yields them a scanty subsistence.

Being a Highlander himself, necessarily acquainted with the manners and customs of his own countrymen, and the Gaelic, his native tongue, he proved a very acceptable itinerant preacher among them, and his Divine Songs have considerably contributed towards his favourable reception. All who have been delighted with them gladly embrace an opportunity of hearing him preach. From these circumstances, the Highlanders are more desirous to attend his preaching than that of a regular minister of any connexion.

There seems to be a striking analogy between his case and that of NATIVE MISSIONARIES in India…Peter Grant must be far more useful in preaching to the Highlanders than any minister or itinerant who, though he may in some measure have acquired their language, is yet , in many respects a stranger to their habits and modes of thinking.

Some of the Independent ministers in the North of Scotland….are anxious that he should be enabled to exert his talents for usefulness in a greater degree than the necessary attention to his farm can at present admit of; and it has been suggested, that a small contribution should be raised by some of those friendly to the Gospel, to enable him occasionally to hire the assistance of a servant upon his farm, and thus afford him more frequent opportunities for itinerating labours.' (the writer goes on to explain the absence of ministers in Highland parishes, the geographical obstacles to church attendance, and the lack of Bibles and any religious instruction). He resumes: 'In such country, how desirable – how unspeakably precious – must a faithful itinerant preacher of the Gospel be? Is he a native who preaches in their mother tongue? One who has spent his life in habits of intimacy and kindness among them? One who has…already succeeded in gaining their grateful admiration and reward? One who is able, ready, and anxious, to labour in the glorious work of declaring the unsearchable riches of the crucified Immanuel? One, above all, of an accredited character – whom judicious Christians of all denominations. agree in recommending to the notice of fellow-Christians, as fit for this great undertaking? If such be the person we have been speaking of, who is there, who has felt the value of the Gospel to his own soul, possessed of a shilling to spare from the luxuries or comforts of life, who will not esteem it a privilege to have an opportunity of diffusing , among the population of a neglected but truly interested district of his native country, the knowledge of that Saviour who alone can recover our guilty race from the ruins of the Fall; and whose word, when believed and rightly understood, is like 'a light shining in a dark place,' sufficient to 'guide their feet into the way of peace – until the day dawn, and the day-star arises.'

The writer of the Memoir gives a specimen of Peter Grant's 'Divine Songs', conceding that 'much is unavoidably lost' in the translation of the poem called 'Calvary'.

'O, poor man, in a natural state,
Who art not in favour with God,
You are pursuing shadows that shall never satisfy your desires.
The law of the Ten Commandments shall not protect you;
Without perfect obedience it never saved any.
But, if you desire salvation, escape from terrific Sinai,
And flee to Mount Calvary.

There you shall see justice a-satisfying, and God making peace!
The Son of His love giving full satisfaction
To preserve us from going down into death.
You shall see there the only substitute,
There was He Himself who bore our sins on the tree;
His wounds and sores shall show His love to His children,
And His resurrection shall convince you of His divinity.

This is the Prince, this is the Saviour,
This is Immanuel Himself,
The Rock of His elect, and strong fort in time of need:
This is He, that giveth salvation to all the seed of Abraham,
And they that drink of His fullness shall be eternally saved.
Ye that spend your store in pursuit of vain pleasures,
Come now, and drink freely of the living water.
My flesh is meat indeed, says the King of glory, to men;
The blood that flowed is a river full of pleasure.'

In his helpful analysis of the themes of 'Dàin Spioradail', Donald Meek takes the over-arching theme of the songs as 'The Glory of the Lamb'. He writes of 'The Lamb – Vision for Mission' , quoting from the 'global' 'Song on the Missionaries'. Professor Meek then pinpoints 'The Lamb – Hope of Salvation' as another of Grant's thematic concerns. The poem 'The Glory of the Lamb' (part of which is quoted above) is a joyful celebration of Christ's triumph over death and His purchasing of salvation.

Peter Grant, however, composed songs aimed at unconverted people. Donald Meek points out that he stresses the comprehensive nature of the atonement, 'as if Grant were particularly concerned to counteract a more limited view of the efficacy of Christ's death. The blood of Christ in its cleansing power is available to all, even though the exercising of mercy rests ultimately in the will and purposes of God.' Grant's song 'The Natural State' says:

'There is breadth and efficacy
in the ransom offered up,
which opened an unobstructed door
for every creature that can move.'

Donald Meek writes: 'The atonement, in Grant's view, was thus sufficient for all who cried out to God....Grant balanced his view of the sufficiency of the atonement with a very clear understanding that sinners had to do something about their lost condition'. Carelessness and indifference are addressed in his hymn 'Calvary' (see extract above), and the fragility of life in this world and the certainty of judgement are set out in his poem 'The Eternal Home':

'As I have been observing the pitiful world,
I have seen it changing hour by hour;
I see people who are now forsaking me,
and going quickly to the eternal home.

Old and young go down to the grave,
Over weak and strong death wins the day;
When their time comes to forsake the world,
Sick or well, they will not get an hour's delay.

But that is a great warning to all the rest;
It is time for me to give it close heed:
It is a grim reminder to prepare to leave it,
Since the earthly house is about to fall....

But when we see, with our temporal eye,
The body returning unto the dust,
The precious soul again makes its way
To receive sentence from the King of All.

Donald Meek's study also highlights 'The Lamb – Focus for Faith's Journey' as one of the dominant themes of Grant's songs, portraying Christians as strangers and pilgrims on the earth, journeying to the heavenly Zion, a place of glorious joy and triumphant music. Songs like 'The Journey' and 'Strangers' take up the themes of the New Testament Letter to the Hebrews chapters 11 and 12.

The good Professor Meek's final theme extracted from Peter Grant's songs is 'The Lamb – Joy beyond Culture' , where he contrasts the Christian's enjoyment of God with the need to reject the lightweight pleasures of contemporary secular culture which provides an empty alternative to the path of the godly life.

These themes are illustrated in two poems. The first, 'The Rejoicing of the Righteous', sets its focus on the Christian's joy, which is not rooted in earthly considerations:

'O, the real joy belongs to those who have knowledge
Of the One so glorious as God's only Son!
Their hope is set, not on things that are fleshly,
But on a crown of glory in the heavenly realm….
Their heart's desire is to be on the far side of Jordan
Singing the song which their devotion knows.'

The second, 'The Complaint of the Gaels', summarises the old life which the Christian Gaels have forsaken:

'And the glorious Sabbath that should be kept holy
Often we spent it foolishly from end to end;
And the most idle talk about Fian warriors,
And every temporal matter that filled our heads…
It was not the Bible that would be proclaimed then,
But an endless, ongoing trivial tale.'

In conclusion, we can say that Peter Grant's overall concern was to create a Christian body of Gaelic verse which would be both popular and practical. To that end, he chose secular tunes (as many others had done before him), to which he set new, spiritual words. These words were carefully chosen according to his 'target audience': he composed songs to encourage Christian believers already on the pathway to the Heavenly City, but he also composed verse to challenge those who were careless about spiritual matters, and required to be 'awakened' to their lost spiritual condition. Above all, he celebrated the joy and freedom which are to be found in Christ. It is an eloquent measure of his success that several of his Gaelic hymns are still sung in the twenty-first century, and that he remains best known, particularly among Gaelic speakers, as a religious poet.

CHAPTER TWELVE –
CHRISTIAN CO-OPERATION

Peter Grant was always keen to relate to his fellow-Christians, near and far. He was particularly keen to work with the small Baptist community in Scotland, and to work for effective partnership in the Gospel among them.

This is not the place to set out in detail the varying influences in Scottish Baptist life from the conversion of the brothers Robert and James Haldane in the mid-1790s until the successful fourth attempt to form a Baptist Union of Scotland in 1869. Dr Brian Talbot has thoroughly and painstakingly set out these factors in his doctoral thesis. We shall just note some of them before setting out the main point of this chapter, that Peter Grant and the Grantown Baptist Church were at the forefront of Scottish Baptist co-operation and Union during most of this period.

The Haldane Brothers came from a family of considerable means, but lost both parents early in life. They sold much of the estate at Airthrey, Stirlingshire, and it is estimated that the Haldanes spent some £70,000 in a ten-year period, promoting Christian causes in Europe, Africa and India – and especially Scotland. The brothers became convinced of the Biblical teaching on believer's baptism, and supported the Baptist cause in Scotland from 1807.

The Haldanes founded a training college with up to sixty students, for whose fees they were responsible. They funded the spread of Bibles and Christian literature, and founded several churches in Scotland. JD Douglas sums them up like this: 'As with his brother James, Robert's social standing opened doors of opportunity, yet his preaching was so simple and direct that it reached the hearts of all kinds of people.'

The Haldanes put their weight behind pan-evangelical co-operation rather than denominational union, but their call to believers to associate, and James' work 'Observations on Forbearance' helped pave the way…

The first Baptist Union of Scotland was formed in May 1827, and attracted the support of about half of the churches, but Brian Talbot says it met its ultimate demise by 1830, mainly due to hesitancies, and criticisms. Grantown-on-Spey Baptist Church was one of the 28 churches who joined. The scant evidence relating to the 1827 Union is found in 'The Waugh Papers'. There were 28 churches within the Union, the most northerly of which were Inverness, John Street, Aberdeen, Academy Street, Aberdeen, and Grantown on Spey. There were 15 member churches of the Scottish Baptist Association (1835-42), including John Street, Aberdeen, Montrose, and Grantown-on-Spey.

Dr Derek Murray has helpfully summarised uniting factors and early attempts at church co-operation. He writes: 'The Haldane Churches were joined in several ways; through the persons of their founders; through their pastors, often Haldane students; through their history; but their association was loose. The Baptist Home Mission churches were linked by their committees, their subscribers, and their annual meetings, but it was not until 1835 that an attempt was made to form a more lasting union.'

In 1827 the church at Grantown was invited to send representatives to Edinburgh, where efforts were being made to form a Baptist Union of Scotland. The invitation came at an awkward time for Peter Grant, who was looking after things until his ordination. Grantown acknowledged the invitation, but did not take part, and the proposed Union did not materialise at that time.

The next attempt to form some such grouping took place in 1835, and resulted in a small group known as The Scottish Baptist Association. Their first meeting took place at Tullymet, where the pastor, Rev Donald Grant, was a former member of the Grantown church. The 'Religious Intelligence' reports on a meeting in Tullymet on 29 July 1835, attended by 'Baptist ministers and brethren'. They had a morning prayer-meeting, and heard 'an excellent and impressive sermon' from James A Haldane of Edinburgh. Letters from various churches and individuals were read, and six resolutions were agreed to, as the framework for ensuing meetings. These were, in summary:

I. They formed a 'Scottish Baptist Association, for churches and members who wished to co-operate'. The list of churches included Grantown, and 9 others.

II. This association envisaged several objects: 1. An increase in brotherly love, friendly intercourse, and evangelistic feeling. 2. The promotion of united exertion to advance Christ's cause and Baptist interests. 3. To gather accurate statistical information relative to Baptist churches and causes. 4. To issue an annual letter to the united churches to report proceedings.

III. To hold an annual meeting at a mutually agreed location, attended by a deputation and a letter from each church. They should report on the work of the past year and show increase, decrease and present actual number, and highlight areas of Scotland with special need of gospel preaching.

IV. No bond is entered into whereby any one church is 'obliged to conform to the usages of the rest'. Any church was to be free to act according to its own views.

The next meeting was to be in Perth in July 1836.

Therefore the personal connection gave a further incentive for the Grantown church to join. The Association was reconstituted as The Baptist Union of Scotland in 1843, with Grantown in membership. During the next few years, the Union became embroiled in controversy, and Peter Grant wrote threatening to resign unless changes were made. The Annual Meeting in August 1848 accepted the resignation with regret. Eight years later the Union was dissolved.

There isn't much evidence concerning inter-denominational relations at Grantown after the initial hostility shown to the Baptists. Probably there was peaceful co-existence, as Baptists and Presbyterians tolerated or ignored one another. In a rural community people have to get along together.

The Church of Scotland had its own big issue to deal with – the Disruption in 1843. This presented the Baptists in Grantown with an interesting situation. A number of people left the parish church to form a local congregation of the Free Church of Scotland. Many of them attended the Baptist services when the newly-formed Free Church had problems caused by a shortage of ministers for the increased number of congregations. The ministers responded to the need by preaching on alternate Sundays. Their congregations had other ideas, and many refused to attend to hear a man not of their variety of Presbyterianism. Consequently, when their minister was away, Peter Grant had a different congregation every week! He seems to have avoided accusations of 'sheep-stealing', and when he was ill some time later, the ministers of the other churches had no problem about supplying his pulpit until he had recovered.

In August 1836, an article was submitted to the Baptist Magazine regarding the state of the Baptist Denomination in Scotland. There was an encouraging meeting in July, involving brethren from a distance of 100 miles, and the gathering 'exhibited a lovely picture' of agreement in the Lord's work. They were encouraged by formation of the Baptist Home Missionary Society, well supported by English Baptists. The writer stoutly defends united efforts in Christian work against suspicions that they are unscriptural. He attempts 'to obviate, as far as possible, objections founded on misconception, or arising from worse motives.' There are minutes for annual meetings of the Baptist Union of Scotland from 1843 to 1847. Peter Grant's letters to his son and successor William give an insight into the controversies during Francis Johnstone's time as secretary of the Union. His book 'The Work of God and the Work of Man in Conversion' displayed what Dr Talbot calls 'formal Arminian, or even Pelagian, sentiments.' He continues '(This work) was a clear condemnation of any form of Calvinism and the traditional Reformed understanding of the work of the Holy Spirit.' In his first Circular Letter as Secretary, the Scottish Baptist Association is renamed as the Baptist Union of Scotland. In the 1850s Calvinistic Baptists were denied access to its life, so they developed affinities with the English Particular Baptists. In the absence of some minutes (1856-1869) for the Scottish Baptist Association, evidence can be gleaned from 'The Freeman', an English Baptist weekly newspaper, and the English Baptist 'Manual of the Baptist Denomination' from 1845-1859, and the Baptist handbook 1861-1879. The strength of Scotch Baptists was sapped in the 1800-1830 period. Dr Brian Talbot comments perceptively, 'The Scotch Baptist tradition had contributed much to Baptist life in Scotland. It was, however, destined to play only a minor part in the future because of disunity within its own ranks.'

Grantown-on-Spey was one of the 38 churches included in the Baptist Union of Scotland from 1843-1856.

Thus, Peter Grant's support for a Union of Baptist Churches was obvious from the outset.

Dr Brian Talbot writes about the Scottish Baptist Association: 'Its slow but steady growth showed that an increased proportion of Baptist churches was convinced of the need for a union of churches. The driving force for this came in 1842, in the form of the afore-mentioned Rev Francis Johnstone, an able and energetic leader, and a second Baptist Union of Scotland was formed in 1843.

Dr Talbot continues: 'The Scotch Itinerant Society, the mission agency of the 'English' Baptists led by George Barclay and Christopher Anderson, merged with the Haldaneite workers in 1824', and this strengthened the mixture. Grantown was also a member church of the Scottish Baptist Association. The third stage of Union was reached in 1843, and lasted until 1856, when Francis Johnstone left Scotland. We needn't spend time documenting issues, but we should note that again Grantown was part of the Union. It came in again when the permanent formation of the Baptist Union of Scotland came about in 1869. Grantown had always given a lead to the Highland Baptist churches.

Peter Grant wrote to his son William, dated 30 March 1846, and quotes from a letter he wrote to James Haldane. In this letter he is explaining his relationship to the Baptist Home Missionary Society and his attitude to the formation of a Scottish Baptist Union:

'Dear Brother Haldane,.........

It is long since I was fully persuaded that divisions, or the want of union, was the chief cause of our Churches making so little progress in Scotland, and this conviction was strengthened by observing that in England, America, West Indies etc where the cause has prospered wonderfully, the generality of Baptists are united in unions or associations, and that the plan has been found to work well for hundreds of years back. Having this conviction, the Committee need not wonder that I should give my countenance to the men who were attempting to remedy the evils I much deplored although their plans would not be altogether what I would wish, still I thought they meant well. I thought I could remain in connection with both, as I was confident that the Union had no intention to hurt the Society, but rather to co-operate with it, and to supply what I thought a great deficiency, that is to supply some of the large towns and some districts of the Low country with Baptist preachers, for which there is great need.

I will therefore tell my mind without reserve, I intend to continue in connection with the Baptist Home Missionary Society as I am, unless they cut me off, but I will not withdraw my name from the Union, until I am convinced that they be so treated.

The letter does not state whether the same message has been sent to all the Highland churches, for I suppose most of them are in connection with the Union, but I will not consult or advise any of them, but simply state my own mind, but I think it would be time enough to send such a message when funds would fail, and when England would cease to support the Society. Then no-one could blame the committee, whatever the result.

I am sorry to be troubling you with so long an Epistle, for I think you will bear me witness that I was not in the habit saying much about myself, but I think necessity is laid upon me just now to say something. Because you wish to know the nature of my connection with the Union, now I am at a loss to know what is meant by this, but if it is a wish to know whether I receive any support from the Union; if that is the meaning, I can say, not one shilling nor any promise or prospect of it, although I am sure the committee was well aware that the few pounds they gave me annually was not sufficient to support me, when every shilling that the church could collect for missionary purposes, or pastoral duties, was sent to themselves. But I never made any complaint, nor did I apply for help to the Union, or any other church or society. I endeavoured to make up the deficiency by working with my own hands, and if now I am cast off in my old age, I can still trust to providence and if the day comes that I cannot dig, I hope I shall not be ashamed to beg.

So I will leave the matter in the hands of the committee, I will not be so unreasonable as the Free Church was once, when they wished support without control, but I hope by the grace of God, no fear of consequences will make me deviate from the path of duty.

But as you have been at so much trouble and expense with the Highland Society, and that the Lord has so signally countenanced and blessed your labour, I think you should ponder well before you would come to such a decision.

You must be better acquainted with the minds of the English Baptists than I can be, and I know that the weight of Scottish Baptists are against the Union, and under this weight the Union may be crushed. But I question much whether the English Baptists would not help you so cheerfully by letting the Union alone.

You will not think from what I have stated, that I approve of the doings of every one connected with the Union. I was sorry for Mr Johnstone going to Edinburgh as I know many other places had need of his labours, and places where he might be more useful. I remonstrated against this, till I was informed that the Union had nothing to do with it, that it was his own personal act.

Wishing the Lord to guide and direct you, I remain yours sincerely,
Peter Grant.'

We noted earlier that Peter Grant had been involved in itinerant ministry. His summer preaching tours had brought him in touch with Independent and Congregational churches, where he preached. At the time of the Disruption in 1843, he allowed the Free Church to share premises to a limited extent. After the Disruption, the Auld Kirk and the Free Church had problems caused by a shortage of ministers for the increased number of congregations.

William Grant, Peter's third son, became his assistant pastor, and this enabled the ageing Peter to divide his responsibilities. William did most of the visits to the outlying districts, while Peter concentrated his efforts on Grantown itself, but there was no slacking off. In 1859, when Peter was 73, father and son were preaching three sermons on Sundays all the year round, and Peter still visited outstations as often as possible. Sunday began with an early morning prayer meeting and exhortation, and closed with a similar gathering after the evening service when the entire congregation remained to take part. On Tuesdays there was a prayer meeting and Bible lecture, and on Thursdays there was a large prayer meeting attended by a good number from other denominations in the town. William's Bible Class for young people had a regular weekly attendance of 70. Outside

Grantown, some out-stations had as many as three prayer meetings each week. Obviously, these were taken by church leaders, but Peter and William attended as often as possible. Until 1866 all baptisms had been conducted in the open air at the River Spey, but on 1 April that year a baptistry was opened in the church and eleven young people were baptized. Most were unusually young, aged between ten and fourteen, but Peter was confident of their conversion, having dealt with each of them himself. Among them was the twelve-year-old son Donald Haldane Grant, a child from his second marriage.

Forty people joined the church in 1866.

Then as now finance could be a problem. The church had been sending contributions to the Baptist Home Mission, who paid Peter, and later William had a small stipend. Peter had never received more than £42 per annum. The old Baptist legendary prayer used to be cynically stated: 'Lord, you keep him humble, and we'll keep him poor!' Growing demands on the Society caused such financial pressures on its resources that there was a question whether they could support two missionaries at Grantown. In 1864 the Grantown church resolved to take full responsibility for Peter's stipend, increasing the amount to £70. The old man, now aged 81, rejoiced at this token of their gratitude for his service.

We may feel that Peter Grant was too holy and dedicated to be approachable. Those who knew him found him an attractive personality to the very end, cheery and kind, with a good sense of humour coupled with a sense of the presence of God. Children enjoyed his company. It came naturally to everyone to think of him as Peter, rather than Mr Grant. He was always interested in fellowship with other Christians who shared the Biblical Gospel.

We can read of Peer's final dispositions regarding the family in the testaments which he executed in December 1865, two years before his death.

'I. the Reverend Peter Grant residing at LynmacGregor Cottage in the Parish of Cromdale find myself at present in perfect soundness of mind, although sometimes frail in body...Therefore, first, as to the concerns of my soul. The Lord having taught me from my youth and helped me to declare His works I heartily confess that I have no hope but in Christ and Him crucified... And, second, whereas my first wife died in the year Eighteen hundred and thirty six, leaving eight children under my charge, whom, under the Blessing and Kind Providence of God, I was able to educate and settle in life, and in the year Eighteen hundred and fifty two, all of my children being married and my small means being disposed of for their benefit and advantage I married my present wife Mrs Janet Grant being at the time in the enjoyment of my salary from the Baptist Home Missionary Society of Scotland but with no other means beyond the little household effects and moveable estate not amounting to twenty Pounds Sterling; and whereas, in or about the year Eighteen hundred and fifty nine I removed from Ballentua where I sometimes resided to my present abode where a house has been build by means of some money belonging to my present wife with assistance from some kind friends on condition that after my death the premises should belong wholly to her. Therefore, and for the love and affection which I have and bear for the said Mrs Janet Grant and for other good causes and considerations I do hereby Give, Grant, Assign and Dispone to the said Mrs Janet Grant....my whole means and Estate....'

Peter Grant would have agreed with the modern slogan: 'Live simply, that others may simply live'. After a frugal life but a happy, hard-working one, he died in the house of LynmacGregor on 14 December 1867, aged 84, having been a preacher for 60 years, and a pastor for 41 years.

His granddaughter Annie and her son JA Grant Robinson tell us of the circumstances in their biographical introduction to the 1926 edition of 'Dain Spioradail'.

Peter Grant, in later life

'The last illness was short. There was no particular disease, just the quiet, painless dissolution of the frame. He knew he was departing. He had no tears, but joyfully looked forward to meeting the Saviour 'Whom, having not seen, he loved.' ….His wife and every one of his children assembled at his bedside. Awaking and seeing them, he had a word for each, and turning to a table loaded with delicacies, grapes and suchlike, sent by many loving friends, he divided a portion to each till the whole was distributed and every hand filled, saying ' – and they were his last words – 'Dainty meat have I given you my children. See that we live in brotherly love, at peace with one another'. Then he turned to the wall and fell asleep in Jesus.'

Worn and frail, he died peacefully, surrounded by his family, preaching, praying and praising to the very end. In our next chapter we shall see how his sowing at Grantown yielded a world-wide harvest.

CHAPTER THIRTEEN –
THE LEGACY, HOME AND OVERSEAS

The Lord blessed the life and ministry of Peter Grant and the Grantown church, like Jacob's prophetic blessing of Joseph in Genesis 49 verse 22: ' Joseph is a fruitful vine, a fruitful vine near a spring, whose branches climb over a wall.' The blessing is intensified in Moses' word to the tribe of Joseph in Deuteronomy 33 verses 13-14: 'May the Lord bless his land with the precious dew from heaven above and with the deep waters that lie below; with the best the sun brings forth, and the finest the moon can yield.' The Hebrew word for blessing is also the word for a knee-joint, and the Jews said that blessing was to the soul what a knee joint was to the body, giving balance, flexibility and resilience to life.

When we try to evaluate God's servants in the past, we have to wonder at their unremitting toil in an unpromising climate, but also the joy God brought into their lives through spiritual and revival blessing in their communities. The influence of the Gospel on Peter Grant and the Grantown church extended initially to his family, and eventually across the world as Christians of Strathspey dispersed into world-wide Christianity. In this chapter we shall attempt to glimpse at least the fringe of this worldwide blessing.

We begin at home, and the influence of the father Peter on his son William, as father discerned the call of God, and encouraged William.

We have three responsibilities in the matter of our God-given gifts and talents. We have to discover them, and then develop them, and finally to use them for the glory of God. In this family, talents, gifts and loving interest were inter-twined.

William was born as the third son of Peter and Ann, on 1 August 1823. He was baptized in 1840, and around that time, aged 16, he was sent to Fortrose in the Black Isle, where the Baptist minister, John Shearer, was conducting training classes for young men.

John Macandrew, a committee member of the Baptist Academical Society for Scotland, heard William preach at Fortrose, and found sponsorship for him to attend two years lectures in Edinburgh, with Dr Chalmers.

His dad wrote him encouraging letters. For example, on 21 December 1843: 'Dear William, May the grace of God that bringeth salvation, be sufficient for you in all that you have to go through. Trust in the Lord forever, for in the Lord Jehovah is everlasting strength. In all thy ways acknowledge Him, and He will direct your paths.
'We received your letter Saturday, glad to hear that the Lord holds your body in health, and your soul in life, and that your studies appear rather to be a pleasure rather than a burden. I was afraid that it might be otherwise after enjoying as long the pleasure of the plough. But Paul learnt in every condition to be content, but this he could only do by Christ strengthening him.'...

On Old Year's Day, 1844: 'My dear William, a happy New Year to you, and much of that grace that makes all things new. I received your letter last week, which makes my heart glad, to find that above all study you are closely studying the Word of God, and that you are not withering like a transplanted tree, which many students do for a while at least, when they begin the study of languages....

'I have no doubt but in due time you will reap a good harvest. I hope you will endeavour gradually to take part in all the services of the sanctuary, although this may lead you into painful feelings at times. Everyone feels less or more of that at first, and some all their days. I still feel much of it, and indeed I think it far better than to be too self-confident. Paul the Apostle of the Gentiles was among the Corinthians in fear and much trembling. So was Moses on the mount.'

Peter writes in a manner reminiscent of Paul to Timothy in a letter dated 3 June 1844: 'Dear William, May Jehovah hold your soul in life and lead you in the way everlasting, with as much earthly comforts as He sees working for His good. I am well in health, and like a text that I got at Fortrose, and from which I preached yesterday, 'Faint but pursuing.'

'Your last letter made me weep for joy, and yet I felt more for you than ever I did, and I wished even more that I had been near you, to relieve your mind ....I gave you too little at home, I did that for the pity I felt for yourself, but it was burying your talent in the earth. However, you will soon regain what you lost by that. Your timidity and fear will be of no loss to you, unless it comes from such a height as to overwhelm you. It will lead you to trust the more to the Lord, it is far better than too much self-confidence… All you have to do is trust in the Lord, to take for your text at first the plainest passages on the Gospel, tho' you may think them too common, they will be quite new for you, and we think more of the lisping of a child, than the oratory of a man… you may consult other men upon your text, they will help you to divide it, and then form your own ideas. They will be more familiar and more natural.'

The Baptist Home Missionary Society sent William to share in the work of Grantown, and he joined his father in the pastorate in 1848.

Peter cannot conceal his joy at William's return, in a letter dated 12 April 1848, addressed care of Mr J Fraser, 1 Scotland Street, Edinburgh: 'Dear William, You may raise your Ebenezer and trust in the Lord forever. There is none in heaven or earth to be desired or trusted like Him…. For the news of your last letter, that home is to be your first settlement, if it was practicable, we would all raise a bonfire on a hill for joy. But at any rate we will confer upon you the freedom of our burgh…I can write only a few lines, which I hope you will have before you leave Edinburgh. Take with you as many books and pamphlets as you can get, and if possible see all your kind friends before you leave town… Let us bless the Lord and exalt his name together.'

In 1845, at the urgent request of his friend Mr Macandrew, William was engaged as an agent of the Home Mission. Mr Macandrew paid the first salary, and secured his protégé other five months at College. When William arrived to share in ministry at Grantown in 1848, he was immediately caught up in the demands and excitement of a local revival. He had already been involved in itinerant preaching in the Strathspey area during his holidays. Now, he took on some responsibility for 'out-stations' – preaching points outwith Grantown, supplied by preachers mainly from the Baptist Church. In August 1848, a work of grace began. And in twenty-one months one hundred converts were baptized and added to the church. The committee of the Home Mission - of which William Grant continued an agent until his father's death in 1867, when he became pastor at Grantown – sent him to preach to the Highland fishermen who gather during the season from all points to Peterhead and Fraserburgh, and he was able to take part in a successful season of soul-winning. His evangelistic work stretched from Huntly to Dingwall, and he preached frequently every day of the week and three times on Lord's days, and this went on for weeks in succession. His labours were much blessed in and around Grantown, especially among young people.

He also took on some Sunday School work, and ran a very successful Bible Class in Grantown. Young people attended in good numbers.

Peter Grant was unwell in the spring of 1862, and William took on most of the work. He put his Gaelic skills, which he had imbibed from his father, to good use in those years.

In the midst of this pressure, 2000 navvies appeared, working on the Perth to Inverness Highland Railway, and the Great North of Scotland line down through Strathspey.

There were real heavyweight forces at work behind the construction of railway lines from Perth to Inverness, first mooted in 1845, and revised by Joseph Mitchell in 1853. The route was to run via Grantown and Aviemore to Inverness.

Two of the major players were John Charles, the seventh Earl of Seafield, and Chief of the Clan Grant, and the seventh Duke of Atholl. Neil Sinclair tells us: 'Five out of the ten largest landowners in the British Isles were on the Board of Directors of the Highland Railway.' (including these two gentlemen). The railway was going to cross their land. Neil Sinclair tells us that the Earl had declined compensation for the intrusion of his grounds, and the railway company built a bridge and lodge two miles north of Grantown where the line crossed the grounds of Castle Grant. These were built by the company in exchange for the Earl's generosity, and provided private access for the Seafield family. The Earl also promoted a huge tree-planting policy (around fifty million trees between 1860 and 1910).

The Duke of Atholl acted to guard his own property and interests, but his support was crucial in the project. The railway company compensated for his concerns and demands by promising to build a new lodge at Blair Castle, to use stone in the building of Blair Atholl station, and to provide compensation for the loss of bridge tolls to and from the bridge at Dunkeld.

Meanwhile, at ground level, we consider the navvies who became a spiritual concern for Peter and William Grant, and the Grantown Baptist church. (a 'navvy' is a colloquial expression for a 'navigator', since they were involved in the back-breaking tasks of making new directions in the building of roads, railways and canals). They lived in cramped, cold, draughty wooden bothies, and were involved in huge physical labour. Two million cubic yards of rock and soil had to be removed and two major bridges constructed. The Culloden Viaduct was 600 yards long and 128 feet above the River Nairn.

The navvies were a mixed multitude – Highland, Lowland, Scottish English and Irish – so there was trouble in the camps. In the miasma of alcoholic celebration on New Year's Day 1862, fighting broke out between the Highland and the Irish navvies, with the Highlanders trying to settle old scores for their scurvy treatment by the Irish and English when building the Hawick railway line.

William set about connecting with the navvies in their camps. So many came to the Baptist Church services, William took to preaching to large congregations in the streets, and doing follow-up work in the mobile camps.

When Peter died in 1867, aged 84, William was called to sole pastorate, when the church took on full responsibility for his stipend of £100 per annum. He was duly inducted on 10 February 1868. He later declined invitations to pastor in Greenock, but in 1870 he went to Edinburgh as one of the pastors of the Scotch Baptist Church at Bristo Place, near George IV Bridge. (The church purchased a new site at Buckingham Terrace, Queensferry Road in 1932). The Scotch Baptists believed in plurality of ministry, so William Grant served with CW Anderson (1868-84), David Kemp (1883-88), A Cromar (1888-1907). William Grant served at Bristo from 1870 until 1902, when he was 79 years old. The Scottish Baptist Magazine article written at his jubilee in ministry said the church numbered 324 members when he came, and now numbered 550. 'He addresses the heart but not at the neglect of the intellect. He possesses too in adequate measure, the pastoral gift, and the sheep are both fed and tended. Visitation is systematically pursued; and long stairs and a widely dispersed membership do not daunt him. Himself a man of tender emotions, he can and does enter into the joys and sorrows of others; and, as in many who feel deeply, a gracious spring of humour lies near the fount of tears.'

Rev Alexander Grant was born in Grantown in 1838. His father was Peter Grant of Achnafearn, and his mother Annie Grant was second daughter and third child of Peter Grant of the Songs. Alexander's maternal grandfather William Macintosh, a farmer in Duthil, was a powerful preacher, notable in the district before the Haldanes began their very influential missionary tours in Scotland. William Macintosh began the first Sabbath School in Strathspey. Alexander's father Peter Grant went to Canada, and was ordained pastor of the Baptist Church at Cumberland, Ontario, serving there until his death. Young Alexander, oldest grandchild of Peter Grant of the Songs, had a special bond with his sister Annie, who was next to him in age in the family. Annie was the first of Peter Grant's grandchildren to be converted. She was baptized on 19 March 1854 in the stream that flows between Grantown and the Highland Railway, a few hundred yards east of the Baptist Church. Peter Grant of the Songs' son and successor William performed the baptism. Alexander Grant's nephew tells how a great crowd gathered on a very frosty morning, and the ice on the pool had to be broken twice, on the previous evening and on the morning of the baptism! Alexander was deeply affected by Annie's confession of faith in Christ, and he was converted at an early age.

He began to preach in his early twenties, and the Scottish Baptist magazine in its 'In Memoriam' article after his death in 1913, tells how he became a self-supporting student for the ministry under the Baptist Association of Scotland. When finishing his course in Glasgow University, Alexander received a call from the Westmoreland Group of Baptist Churches to assist their godly elderly pastor, John Fawcett, with whom he served for almost seven years. He moved to Anstruther Baptist Church where he was minister from 1871-1878. The membership doubled and a fine manse was built during those years. He became co-pastor with Rev Robert Watson in John Street Baptist Church, Glasgow, from 1878-1885, and was the chosen Convener of the Baptist Union's Education Committee.

His wife's poor health demanded a change of climate. The family (six persons including himself) moved to Santa Barbara, California, USA, in 1888, where he laboured for twelve years from 1889 as pastor of the Santa Barbara Baptist Church. He was a strong and energetic leader, eager to promote evangelistic preaching and temperance causes. He became one of the denominational leaders, and was influential in the formation of the Baptist Convention of Southern California. He was appointed as the Convention's first President, and was retained on the active directorate until his death on 18 May 1913. One of his American brethren said 'he had a heart as large as a barn door', and preached constantly until his final illness. The obituary notice in the Santa Barbara Morning Press of 20 May 1913 mentions his three ministerial brothers, Rev Peter Grant and Rev Donald Grant of California, and Rev James Grant of Connecticut.

If the definition of God-given revival includes significant long-term effects beyond the boundaries where it started, God's continued blessing of the Grants' ministry certainly fits the bill.

A number of Grantown men went into what used to be called 'full-time Christian service', home and abroad. They took the aroma of Christ and the fervour of Lachlan Macintosh and Peter Grant with them. The men we can mention here included nearly twenty from William Grant's Bible Class! Here is a sample:

William Tulloch's activities date from the days of the fierce MacShimidh in Grantown. He spent many years at Blair Atholl, from 1819 until 1861. He wrote a book on 'Itinerating Exertions in the Highlands.'

We have given detailed mention of Duncan Dunbar, who served God as pastor at New Brunswick and New York.

There were three Alexander Grants worthy of mention. One served at London Baptist Church, Ontario, Canada.

Another was minister of John Street, Glasgow, 1878-85.

The third was based at Tobermory until 1873, and did pioneer work on Mull and the Inner Islands. He travelled to Ireland to observe the progress of the 1859 revival in Ulster, and prayer meetings and lectures on revival were organised on his return. His work gave a fresh impetus to the movement of the Holy Spirit in the churches of the island churches since the early 1840s and in the late 1850s and early 1860s.

James McQueen was the tireless minister at Broadford in Skye. He died of smallpox contracted during his pastoral work among the sufferers.

John Watson became Minister of Cadgee Baptist Church in New South Wales, Australia.

Several men from Grantown became Baptist ministers in Canada. Donald Meek comments that 'these emigrant preachers cannot be regarded as direct leaders of the emigrant movement, although their removal to Canada strengthened the new emigrant communities.' The movement west to Canada was due to a complex of factors, including starvation in Scotland, the Highland Clearances, the 'call of the wild' wrapped up in the call of God, and the 'Macedonian call' (Acts 16 verse 9) of Scottish emigrants in Canada.

Baptist pastors, and other non-Established church pastors without the security of manses and glebes, and better financial security, were more likely to emigrate. The Baptist Home Missionary Society for Scotland's report of 1839 contains a letter from a Baptist pastor, which includes the following: 'I have always discouraged emigration from fear of making desolation in our pleasant church, as it has done in many other Highland churches; but I fear it will not do any longer, and that pinching poverty will force many of our dear brethren to leave the bosom of the church where they wished to live and die, and to seek a livelihood in some other region.' Sometimes the movement to the New World involved more specific factors like the failure of the potato crop from 1836 into the 'hungry forties', which, again, was viewed as part of God's providential leading.

William Fraser settled at Kincardine, Ontario, on the shore of Lake Huron. William Fraser deserves some detailed mention. He was born in 1801, converted in 1817 through the preaching of Peter Grant in Grantown, and was baptized by Lachlan Mackintosh. He attended Robert Haldane's college, and began itinerant preaching in 1825. By 1825 he was pastor in Uig, Skye, and was set apart formally in July 1828 in the presence of Walter Munro of Fortrose, Alexander Grant of Tobermory and Dugald Sinclair of Lochgilphead. He was approached by the church in Breadalbane, Glengarry County, Ontario, and emigrated in 1831. There was a substantial group of Highland emigrants in the area.

This Gaelic-speaking Highlander was described as a physical and spiritual giant of herculean stature, like Apollos in the Scriptures - 'a man mighty in the Scriptures', a strong leader. He acquired a small farm, and was supported for some time by the Baptist missionary Society of New York. He saw a revival movement of the Holy Spirit in Breadalbane after an unpromising beginning, and as a seasoned itinerant preacher trained in the Highlands, Donald Meek writes that he travelled widely in Eastern Ontario and Quebec, and stimulated and encouraged several churches. In Breadalbane, he worked as an evangelist, and acted as superintendent of public schools.

Donald Meek tells us that in 1850, 'he (Fraser) moved west to Bruce County, Ontario, where he was instrumental in founding the Baptist Church at Tiverton, where he exercised a powerful ministry for 25 years. After his 'retirement' in 1881 (aged 80) he travelled to Manitoba 'with the hope of finding enough Highlanders someplace to form a congregation.' William Fraser was like Mallory and Irvine on Mount Everest; 'when last seen, they were still climbing'.

In the publication 'Sketches of Canadian Baptists' William Tulloch includes 'Sketch' written by Rev William Fraser, aged 77, who spent 46 of his 58 years in ministry, in Canada. Rev William Fraser, pastor at Collingwood, Ontario, writes:

My first charge was in the county of Glengarry, Breadalbane, 50 miles above Montreal. There I found a church of 31 memebers, with whom I laboured 19 years. There are now between 200 and 300 communicants, and a large congregation, with a stated ministry; a fine stone chapel, a good brick manse, and a glebe of 20 acres of good clear land. On the field of my missionary labour, there are now 18 Baptist churches, a number of them with large memberships and very fine chapels....In the year 1850 I went about 400 miles further back into the country, to Tiverton, County of Bruce. In that new county I laboured five years preparing materials. On 4 June 1855, we founded a church of 24 members, laboured among them for 20 years, and resigned my charge eighteen months ago from infirmity and age, and now live with my daughter, Mrs Coutts. Her husband, Mr Coutts was my helper and co-pastor for five years in Tiverton, and is now pastor of the Baptist church of this new and rising town of Collingwood. He left Tiverton for want of Gaelic, which is required there, though not here.

Yet in the mountains around Collingwood, I found no small demand on my Gaelic. In one glen I found 19 Baptists as sheep without a shepherd – all Gaelic-speaking people; and in a large congregation there was only one man who could not understand Gaelic. Preaching again next day, no English was required. On the very top of the highest mountain, 1600 feet above the lake, there is a fine settlement, 4 miles by six, with a chapel and school-house. I have preached different times, both in English and Gaelic. In leaving Tiverton, I never thought my Gaelic would be in so much request elsewhere in Canada. The very best of land is found in the mountains, the purest air and water; and they are studded with farms and houses. The value of the mountains being discovered, many of the Gaels from their native Highland homes poured in; and they are now well off, or on the way of being so.

The Baptist church of Tiverton was the first Baptist church of the county of Bruce, and now numbers more than 400 members, after swarming three times. Towards the formation of one church last year they dismissed 100 members; towards another this year, 12 more; and towards another, before either of these, 31, which has since risen to 100. There is now in the county a population of 56,000, with 17 Baptist churches; while two years previous to my getting there, all was wild Indian territory, and an unbroken forest without a settler!

James Grant ministered at Paris, on the Grand River, Ontario.

Peter Grant served at Cumberland, British Columbia.

James Johnstone served as a missionary in Jamaica.

Alexander Young was minister at Elgin (1877-81).

James McGregor gathered a nucleus in Hopeman, which led to the founding of the Baptist Church there.

Daniel Grant served as minister at Tullymet for many years (1839-84).

Alexander Thomas was an elder from 1852-75 at Stirling Street, Galashiels, which retained the Scotch Baptist plurality of ministry.

He became pastor of the group which formed the Baptist Church in Stirling Street, Galashiels, from 1875 until 1908.

FWC Bruce served at Baptist Churches at Liverpool and Cradley Heath.

Francis Macintosh was minister at Dunfermline Viewfield.

John Fisher commented: 'Those of you who know Grantown today may feel it is a quiet backwater. It was not always so….'

Memorial plaque in Grantown-on-Spey Baptist Church

POSTSCRIPT

When Gladys Aylward, the 'Small Woman', and missionary in China, was leading about 100 orphans to freedom across the Yellow River, they reached an impasse. They were fleeing from the Japanese invasion of China. They arrived at the Yellow River, and the ferry that had been promised was nowhere to be seen. The Japanese forces advancing west could appear at any time, and Gladys wondered what to do.

One of the children suggested she should hold her walking stick over the river, like Moses did with the Red Sea, and the waters would part. Gladys said 'But I'm not Moses!', and the child said 'But God is still God!' The ferryman came and they were all delivered safely on the other side.

Christians today are facing an invasion. Sometimes nations get what they deserve, or even what they want. Old, hard-won standards of Christian heritage are disappearing. As I write, the Scottish Government seem to be blithely ignoring the results of a confrontation regarding the re-definition of marriage. Our dear Church of Scotland friends are in turmoil over single-sex marriage. Christianity is so weak, and the forces of secular humanism seem so rampant. Other religions seem to be doing well. This week I heard on the BBC that 100,000 people a year in Britain are converting to Islam. Christian churches are closing all over the place, and some of them have re-invented themselves into becoming variety playhouses. Our children and grandchildren in school are being exposed to a tide of damaging literature. Good people seem to be getting hounded in 'Christian-bashing' exercises in the law-courts of the land.

Some would ask what is the point of writing about a Highland farmer who lived long ago and far away? The answer would probably lie in the value of taking stock of our past, and reminding ourselves that God is still God. He understands all the forces at work in our lives, just as He did in the Highlands where Peter Grant lived, long ago.. It would be unrealistic to expect Him to act exactly as he did in Grantown. But there are still many people who long that He would be merciful to us today. We long and pray that He would move again in a contextually valid revival which will give honour and glory to His Name, His Son, and His Good News.

APPENDIX –
THE ORIGINS OF THE
GRANTOWN-ON-SPEY BAPTIST CHURCH

We shall gather some events and evidence cited earlier, but viewed in relation to the formation of the Grantown-on-Spey Baptist Church, and the activities of its minister, Rev Peter Grant.

The origins of the Grantown-on-Spey Baptist Church were set out by William Grant, third son of Peter Grant of the Songs, and third pastor, on 1st June 1889. He did this 'to supply the want of a regular Church Book,' and I will summarise his account. William did not paint a rosy picture. He said that 'The whole country was sunk in deplorable ignorance, and profligacy. Its ministers were thoroughly legal in their preaching, and worldly in their lives. The first to disturb that situation was William Macintosh, his maternal grandfather, whose daughter Anne married Peter Grant. William Macintosh preached house to house, and also in the grounds of Established church, as the congregation were leaving. His audience included the astonished minister! At length the people built a turf meeting house for him above Tulloch Farm, at Tullochgoram. When the minister's interest was replaced by hostility, he apparently instigated the burning down of the turf meeting-house.

The Haldane brothers encouraged and, through the Society for Propagating the Gospel at Home, financed itinerant preachers like John Ferguson to work in the area. Peter Grant wrote about Him about forty years later: 'His (Ferguson's) doctrine was new, and fell like thunder on people's consciences.' A local farmer called MacShimidh, an uncultured man with a rough voice, was stirred in spirit by Ferguson's message, and began to preach about sin and divine judgement in the open air, and in churchyards as people were leaving service.

John Reid, a preacher from Haldane's Society for Propagating the Gospel at Home, instigated the formation of Rothiemurchus Congregational Church in 1805, with about thirty members. People from Strathspey and Badenoch travelled there, where Lachlan Macintosh, a native of Badenoch led the congregation. There wasn't much evangelical competition. The parish minister at Abernethy, six miles away from Grantown, would say at sermon time in the service: 'Let us hear what Boney (Napoleon Bonaparte) is doing now', and would spend the time reading news of the Napoleonic Wars from the newspaper to the congregation.

William Grant wrote that Lachlan Macintosh was 'conspicuous among them for gifts and force of character.'

Because of the distance people travelled to the services, and the increasing numbers, the church agreed to divide into two groups, one at Rothiemurchus, and one at Grantown, with 'mutual fellowship and harmony.' In other words, the Grantown church was a plant rather than a split, an extension church rather than an ex-tension church. (Grant Robinson argued, unconvincingly, that the infant baptism issue arose before Lachlan Macintosh settled in Grantown, and that this was the reason for his leaving Rothiemurchus).

Lachlan Macintosh was to concentrate on Grantown, where he was known initially as 'The Missionary'.

Alexander Haldane tells how part of the Haldane money was used to fund seminary teaching in a series of nine classes initially, mainly in Edinburgh, Glasgow and Dundee. There were others, in Grantown, where Lachlan Macintosh led from 1820, and in Elgin. The courses lasted two years, and covered English grammar and rhetoric, the elements of Greek and Hebrew, systematic theology, and essays on additional subjects. We cannot overstate the generosity of James Haldane in the training and funding of preaching. Macintosh chided those who had been at the receiving end of his great kindness, and then regarded his fortune 'as a wreck cast upon a shore, to which all ought to be allowed to help themselves.'

Lachlan Macintosh hit a problem at Grantown. The itinerant preacher was asked to baptize an infant, the child of a church member. He replied: 'Really, you must teach me how to do it. I see no example for it, and do not in the world know how to do it.' Challenged on the matter, he denied the validity of infant baptism, and the matter was referred to James Haldane. At Haldane's request, Macintosh walked to Edinburgh, fully expecting that Haldane would produce evidence to prove conclusively that he had misunderstood the situation. In fact, the reverse happened, and after thorough study and discussion, first Macintosh, and then a month later, the Haldanes were both baptized as believers. From then on, Haldane's resources were used to promote Gospel preaching on Baptist lines.

On his return to Grantown, Macintosh offered his resignation as pastor, but after careful discussion the little church declined to accept it. Instead, they accepted the doctrine of believers' baptism as Scriptural, and were baptized in the River Spey. Seven were then formed into Grantown Baptist Church at a meeting held in Alexander Grant's house at Angach, near the old Spey Bridge Grantown Baptist Church was formed around 1805, with seven members. Their earliest meeting-place was in the home of Alexander Grant (one of the members), who fitted up a room for the purpose at home in Angach, on the left bank of the Spey, a few hundred yards lower down than General Wade's Bridge near Grantown. Robert Grant of Muckerach, opening a Grantown sale of work, said he could not recall the old church of the day, 'but it was originally a dwelling-house to which was subsequently added a wing or gable.'

Lachlan Macintosh was set apart as the first pastor. He was supported partly by Mr Haldane and partly by his own efforts in teaching school. William Grant wrote: 'L. Macintosh was away beyond his fellow countrymen in natural endowments and vocational acquirements remarkably fitted to communicate his knowledge in private, and in powerful public preaching.'

Two tasks now lay before the infant church. The first was to gain acceptance in the community when the factor was decidedly hostile, and the second was to overcome the financial pressures on the pastor. Robert Grant of Muckerach says: 'The congregation increased in spite of considerable opposition and ridicule on the part of the other inhabitants.'

In the early days, it seems the Earl of Seafield's factor was unhelpful, but it seems threats of eviction for any tenant who invited Lachlan Macintosh to conduct a service in a house were not carried out. The pastor managed to obtain his own house in Grantown. Some of Macintosh's preaching was done in a gravel-pit, and hundreds attended on Sunday afternoons.

The congregation worshipped under primitive conditions. Joining the church as a baptized believer was also somewhat primitive and demanding. The baptisms were conducted in a deep sandy pool on the River Spey near the end of the new road. The candidates were immersed in the river, often in winter, often in ice and snow. In those days it was a threefold immersion, in the Name of the Father , the Son, and the Holy Spirit. The candidates had to walk back to the church in dripping garments. It required a hardy constitution to stand such an ordeal. JA Grant Robinson wrote in 1913 of how his mother, Peter Grant's grandchild Annie, was baptized in the River Spey on 19 March 1854, and the Highland weather was such that men with axes broke the ice on the pool the night before her baptism, and the pool had frozen over by the next morning, when the axe-men were at work again! Peter preached the sermon, and his son William went into the icy water to conduct the baptism.

Public baptisms often attracted huge crowds, and elicited varied reactions, ranging from amusement to ridicule. Estimates of the number attending ranged as high as a thousand, or twelve hundred, or two thousand. The Inverness Advertiser of 21 March 1865 reported on baptisms conducted by Peter Grant in the River Ness.

'Another of those unwonted baptism spectacles, the first of which attracted so much attention here in mid-winter, was seen on Sabbath last, the weather again being cold and unpropitious. The time selected for the display was about one o'clock, which being the hour of dismissal from the forenoon service in the churches, was thus well calculated to ensure publicity by gathering together an immense crowd of onlookers. As on the former occasion, the spot chosen was the river bank at Ness House, and the proceedings being visible from the Suspension Bridge, as well as from the opposite side of the stream and the Castlehill, a dense mass of wondering spectators, numbering probably about 2000, were assembled at every available point to witness the proceedings. The Rev.Mr Grant, Baptist minister, Grantown, officiated in the present instance. He gave a rather lengthy discourse, the purport of which could only be ascertained by those in his immediate vicinity, and then offering up prayer, the rev gentleman descended the steps leading to the water, and taking one of the two young females who had been sitting there by the hand, the two walked boldly into the Ness until the rev. gentleman was nearly up to the knees. The placing one arm around the girl's neck, and laying the other hand on her breast, he let her gently down into the water, into which she disappeared for a moment. On emerging, and regaining her feet –somewhat bewildered looking, it must be confessed – the clergyman said a few words , and led the dripping damsel back to the river bank. A general laugh from the spectators when the 'dip' was made, appeared to express their appreciation of the extreme ludicrousness of the spectacle. The same process being gone through with another girl, the ceremonial of the day was brought to a conclusion. Cabs were in waiting to receive the young women, who were driven off with the rev. gentleman and their friends amidst considerable noise and bustle, the crowd pressing forward to get a near look at the courageous damsels and their draggled garments. As to the propriety or otherwise of such exhibitions we say nothing, as they seem to be made matter of conscience with many good people; it may not be out of our province, however, to repeat a former suggestion that neither the time nor the place was very judiciously chosen. If baptisms must, in the opinion of some persons, take place in the open air, and in a running water, they may surely be conducted in some quieter spot than the very centre of a town and at a time when the largest crowd is sure to be gathered together. In this latter there is always an element of danger, and we confess it was not without some trepidation that we saw some thousand persons hanging towards one side of the Suspension Bridge on Sabbath. Very probably the bridge may be able to bear such a strain and much more, but in the interest of the public we beg to suggest that, in case there is any repetition of such observances in the same place – which the good sense of the parties should lead them to avoid – the magistrates should make it a point to see that the bridge is kept clear of crowding.'

In course of time, Lachlan Macintosh had six children, and the cost of living in wartime, and the poor offerings in the period afterwards brought hardship.

Around 1812 Lachlan Macintosh and Peter Grant were reading some poetry, and Macintosh suggested that they should try which of them could make the best poem in Gaelic, and take Dugald Buchanan's poems for their model. 'We took a week to compose the poems, and when they appeared, mine was the best.' This set Peter off writing poems, and eventually he published them Haldane's allowance was only forty pounds a year. His situation was probably eased when he took up teaching in the Haldane seminary from 1820, but the problem would not go away, and as a result Macintosh left Grantown for Dundee in 1826. His situation was exacerbated because of several members being excommunicated.

He was pastor of Orangefield Baptist Church, Greenock from 1829-32, but returned to the North, serving for the next twenty years as the Travelling Agent of the Baptist Home missionary Society for Scotland. He had prior experience as an itinerant preacher, walking great distances, and preaching frequently. On 4 June 1818 he wrote a report for James Haldane about a preaching tour which lasted from 15 April until the middle of May, visiting Cullen, Boyndie, Aberchirder, Banff, Portsoy, Whitehills, Balmaud, Fraserburgh, Inverallochy and St Combs. He had served Grantown well. The little church of seven members now numbered 74, and there was no church minute book. After he left, the congregation called Peter Grant to be pastor. He was reluctant to accept the call. They could have called someone else, but they could not support him. Peter accepted, promising to do what he could for a time, and support himself the best way he could from his farm. He was allowed to retain his own views as a free communionist, and he agreed not to seek to bring any into the church who had not been baptized by immersion.

The witnessed copy of the lease document drawn up on 5 October 1857 names the parties to the lease as 'the Right Honourable John Charles Earl of Seafield, heritable proprietor of the subject after described, n the one part, and Peter Grant, Minister of the Gospel residing at Ballentua near Grantown, William Grant, minister of the Gospel residing at Grantown aforesaid, James Grant, merchant there, John Grant, farmer, Bacharn near Grantown, Peter Grant, farmer, Auchnafairn, Alexander McGregor, farmer, Cottartown, William McGregor, farmer, Auchnarrow, all near Grantown aforesaid, James Finlay Junior, baker, Grantown, and Allan Grant, merchant there, as trustees….

'the trustees shall hold, and manage the said subjects in trust for behoof of the said Baptist Church and for the present and future members of the same….

'trustees are bound to pay all taxations and any public burdens…
'buildings erected… shall not be used or applied for any other purposes than those that are herein before specified (as a chapel and place of worship).

There is an interesting report on Grantown Baptist Church life in an

Appendix by the Commissioners of Religious Instruction, Scotland, for the Presbytery of Abernethy and the Presbytery of Forres, which were visited on 9 September 1837. This states that Rev Peter Grant had been minister for 10 years. 'The congregation belongs to the particular or Calvinistic Baptists, and was first established in the parish in 1806. The average attendance was about 230, and the total attending about 250. The numbers had been increasing till 1835. The minister states that the whole under his charge consisted of 128 communicants, and 86 stated hearers. The maximum number of members was 292.

Nearly the whole are of the poor and working classes, and collections by the hearers amount to about five pounds per annum.

The collection by the communicants are given generally to the congregation. The collection by the hearers are given to the Home Missionary Society for Scotland.

The congregation assembles in a private house, enlarged and fitted up for a chapel. It is the private property of the minister, and is applied to no other purpose. It originally cost £80, and was fitted up as a chapel in the year 1828, at the expense of £40, paid for by subscriptions from the hearers at different times. It is free of debt.

Fourteen inhabited dwelling-houses, occupied by members of the congregation, are more than two miles from the place of worship; six more than six miles; and a few as far as fifteen miles.

Places in the church are stated to be free to the poor as well as the rich. The minister receives £20 annually from the Baptist Home Missionary Society, and states that he supports his family by cultivation of a small farm, held on lease. He has no security for his salary.

On each Sabbath, three sermons and one lecture are delivered in the chapel, and a Sabbath School is taught. There is one fellowship meeting on a weekday, beside occasional services by the minister and others.

He also preaches once a week in different places in the surrounding country, to all who may be inclined to hear.

He extends his exertions to the distance of 15 miles, and sometimes to the distance of 20 or 30.

He preaches in private houses, or in the fields, as circumstances admit, and has done so, less or more, for 26 years.'

ABOUT THE AUTHOR

George is a Glaswegian who was converted and trained for service at Lambhill Evangelical Church, Glasgow, and London Bible College (now London School of Theology). He worked for five years as a metallurgist with Colvilles Limited, an iron and steel manufacturer, and since his call to ministry has served as a Baptist Pastor in Scotland for 21 years, a lecturer in Old Testament and Hebrew Studies at the Bible Training Institute, Glasgow for five years, and principal RE teacher for ten of his twelve years at a 1000-pupil comprehensive school in Glasgow's east end.

He was President of the Baptist Union of Scotland 1995-96, and has written several books, including 'Comfy Glasgow', 'Revival Man – the Jock Troup Story', and study books on Galatians and Philippians. He ministers as far afield as Tenerife and Kenya.

He plays golf and badminton, and plays tuba and flugelhorn.

George has been married to Jean for 48 years, and they have two married children, Finlay and Janet, and two grandchildren, Kirstin and Angus. George is deeply grateful for the Lord's grace and Jean's patience.